Dollars *and Sense*

The Nonprofit Board's Guide to Determining Chief Executive Compensation

by Brian H. Vogel and Charles W. Quatt

BOARDSOURCE
Building Effective Nonprofit Boards

Quatt ASSOCIATES

Library of Congress Cataloging-in-Publication Data

Vogel, Brian H.

  Dollars and sense : the nonprofit board's guide to determining chief executive compensation / by Brian H. Vogel and Charles W. Quatt.

   p. cm.

   Includes bibliographical references and index.

   ISBN 1-58686-088-7 (pbk. : alk. paper) 1. Chief executive officers--Salaries, etc. 2. Nonprofit organizations--Management. 3. Compensation management. I. Quatt, Charles W. II. Title.

   HD4965.2.V64 2005
   658.4'072--dc22

                                                                    2005005816

Published by BoardSource
1828 L Street, NW, Suite 900
Washington, DC 20036

BoardSource, formerly the National Center for Nonprofit Boards, is the premier resource for practical information, tools and best practices, training, and leadership development for board members of nonprofit organizations worldwide. Through our highly acclaimed programs and services, BoardSource enables organizations to fulfill their missions by helping build strong and effective nonprofit boards.

BoardSource provides assistance and resources to nonprofit leaders through workshops, training, and our extensive Web site, www.boardsource.org. A team of BoardSource governance consultants works directly with nonprofit leaders to design specialized solutions to meet organizations' needs and assists nongovernmental organizations around the world through partnerships and capacity building. As the world's largest, most comprehensive publisher of materials on nonprofit governance, BoardSource offers a wide selection of books, videotapes, CDs, and online tools. BoardSource also hosts the BoardSource Leadership Forum, bringing together governance experts, board members, and chief executives of nonprofit organizations from around the world.

Created out of the nonprofit sector's critical need for governance guidance and expertise, BoardSource is a 501(c)(3) nonprofit organization that has provided practical solutions to nonprofit organizations of all sizes in diverse communities. In 2001, BoardSource changed its name from the National Center for Nonprofit Boards to better reflect its mission. Today, BoardSource has approximately 8,000 members and has served more than 75,000 nonprofit leaders.

For more information, please visit our Web site, www.boardsource.org, e-mail us at mail@boardsource.org, or call us at 800-883-6262.

Have You Used These BoardSource Resources?

VIDEOS

Meeting the Challenge: An Orientation to Nonprofit Board Service

Speaking of Money: A Guide to Fundraising for Nonprofit Board Members

BOOKS

The Board Chair Handbook

Managing Conflicts of Interest: Practical Guidelines for Nonprofit Boards

Driving Strategic Planning: A Nonprofit Executive's Guide

The Board-Savvy CEO: How To Build a Strong, Positive Relationship with Your Board

Presenting: Board Orientation

Presenting: Nonprofit Financials

Meet Smarter: A Guide to Better Nonprofit Board Meetings

The Board Building Cycle: Nine Steps to Finding, Recruiting, and Engaging Nonprofit Board Members

The Policy Sampler: A Resource for Nonprofit Boards

To Go Forward, Retreat! The Board Retreat Handbook

Nonprofit Board Answer Book: Practical Guide for Board Members and Chief Executives

Nonprofit Board Answer Book II: Beyond the Basics

The Nonprofit Legal Landscape

Self-Assessment for Nonprofit Governing Boards

Assessment of the Chief Executive

Fearless Fundraising

The Nonprofit Board's Guide to Bylaws

Understanding Nonprofit Financial Statements

Transforming Board Structure: New Possibilities for Committees and Task Forces

THE GOVERNANCE SERIES

1. *Ten Basic Responsibilities of Nonprofit Boards*
2. *Financial Responsibilities of Nonprofit Boards*
3. *Structures and Practices of Nonprofit Boards*
4. *Fundraising Responsibilities of Nonprofit Boards*
5. *Legal Responsibilities of Nonprofit Boards*
6. *The Nonprofit Board's Role in Setting and Advancing the Mission*
7. *The Nonprofit Board's Role in Planning and Evaluation*
8. *How To Help Your Board Govern More and Manage Less*
9. *Leadership Roles in Nonprofit Governance*

For an up-to-date list of publications and information about current prices, membership, and other services, please call BoardSource at 800-883-6262 or visit our Web site at www.boardsource.org.

Contents

Acknowledgments ix

Introduction x

Chapter 1: Understanding the Board's Role in Setting Chief Executive Compensation 1

Chapter 2: Aligning Compensation with Organizational Mission, Goals, and Culture 5

   Measuring Performance: The Balanced Scorecard Approach....5

   Understanding Organizational Culture 6

Chapter 3: Outlining the Title, Job Description, and Profile.........9

   Major Elements of a Chief Executive Job Description...........10

Chapter 4: Developing a Compensation Philosophy 14

Chapter 5: Understanding the Marketplace 17

   The Nonprofit Marketplace 17

   The Organization's Specific Marketplace 18

   Sources of Market Information..19

      IRS 990 Data...20

      Publicly Available Surveys 20

         Understanding and Using Survey Data........................22

         Aging the Survey Data 24

      Special Surveys 24

Chapter 6: Meeting the Legal Standards....................................25

   Private Inurement..25

   Intermediate Sanctions 26

      Revenue Sharing, Incentives, and Bonuses 28

      Initial Contract Exception 28

      The Rebuttable Presumption of Reasonableness 28

      A Second Protection from Personal Liability 30

   IRS Form 990 Reporting..30

   Complying with State Law 31

   The Importance of Legal Counsel 31

Chapter 7: Passing the Test of Public and Stakeholder Scrutiny...32

   Internal Stakeholders: The Staff 33

   What Is the Public Perception? 34

Chapter 8: Understanding the Elements of Compensation 36

   Base Salary and Annual Salary Adjustments 36

   Bonuses, Incentives, and Other Annual Cash Compensation Awards 39

Sign-On and Retention Bonuses 41

Deferred Compensation 44

    Tax-Deferred Compensation 44

        457(b) Plans 45

        457(f) Plans 46

    Split Dollar Life Insurance Plans 46

Other Benefits and Perquisites 47

The Final Compensation Package 49

Chapter 9: Term Negotiations and Final Contracts 50

Negotiating Employment Terms 50

Writing the Employment Contract 54

Severance 56

Conclusion 58

Appendix I: Using Consultants 60

Appendix II: Sample Chief Executive Contract 62

Appendix III: FAQs 66

General Topics 66

   What are the trends towards making nonprofit salaries
competitive? 66

   What issues that nonprofits face in compensation are the same
as or different from those that for-profits face? 66

   How do nonprofits determine salaries for chief executives? 66

   How does budget size relate to the chief executive's salary? 67

Board Responsibility 67

   Should the entire board be aware of and/or approve the chief
executive's salary and benefits each year? 67

   Our board has not historically approved the chief executive's
salary and benefit package. We currently do not know specifics,
so we need to get that information. Is it acceptable to ask the
director to give us his salary, cost of health insurance, pension,
and other information? 67

   Can the board limit what it is willing to pay for a chief
executive position and indicate that certain benefits are not
negotiable? 67

Legal Issues 68

   Which laws should the board be familiar with when setting the
chief executive's salary? 68

   What is the IRS text on intermediate sanctions? 68

   Are 501(c)(6) organizations included in intermediate
sanctions? 68

Are chief executive pay records public information? What about the pay of other employees? 68

Overall Compensation 68

How much money should a chief executive make? Should it exceed the combined salaries of the rest of the employees? 68

Can you give me a list of the common compensation surveys? 69

Performance Evaluation and Incentive-Based Compensation 69

We are in the process of evaluating our chief executive. How do we link this to compensation? 69

Is incentive-based compensation for the chief executive of a nonprofit legal? 69

My board chair and I would like to know what is common practice, or what options exist, for building in merit raises/bonuses for chief executive contracts. How do other nonprofits handle this? Is it put in the contract? Is it tied to performance? 69

Is it common, or ethical, for the chief executive to receive incentive compensation based on the amount of money brought in? 70

Our chief executive is compensated by percentage of revenue; the salary is getting out of hand. What is a legal cap on executive compensation? 70

Benefits 70

I think our chief executive receives too many benefits. How can I determine this? 70

Do nonprofits offer sabbaticals? 71

Our organization provides an automobile for the chief executive, which she is able to use for her private needs as well. Is this acceptable? 71

Should we provide a small mortgage to our chief executive? 71

Do you have any statistics on severance pay agreements? 71

Are signing bonuses frowned upon by donors, the IRS, or others? Can we hire someone at $65,000 per year and give him or her half up front and the rest later as a regular pay? 71

Contracting 71

What are the advantages/disadvantages of chief executive employment contracts? How common is the practice? What should be included? What should be the duration? 71

Do chief executives negotiate? 72

Appendix IV: Glossary of Terms **73**

Suggested Resources **77**

Organizations 77

General Survey Data 77

Regional Survey Data 78

Surveys of Specific Types of Nonprofits 79

    Education 79

    Museums 79

    Philanthropic Organizations.. 79

    Trade Associations 79

Publications 80

About the Authors **82**

LIST OF BOXES

Checklist for Establishing a Chief Executive
Compensation Plan 3

Questionnaire 1: What Are the Major Responsibilities of the
Chief Executive in Meeting Organizational Challenges? 11

Questionnaire 2: What Characteristics Are Most Important
for Consideration in Finding the Right Chief Executive? 13

Sample Compensation Philosophy 16

Factors To Consider When Defining Your Organization's
Marketplace 19

Salary Survey Data 23

What Should Committee Members Consider When
Planning a Compensation Package? 35

Determining If Extra Cash Compensation Makes Sense
for the Organization 41

Setting Up a Bonus or Incentive Program 42

List of Benefits Options for Chief Executives 48

Negotiating Employment Terms.. 50

Elements To Include in an Employment Contract for Chief
Executives.. 55

Acknowledgments

The authors would like to thank first the staff at BoardSource — Marla Bobowick, who first suggested to Charlie Quatt that we write a piece on chief executive compensation; Claire Perella, who managed the writing and editing process; and our editor Deborah Kennedy.

For their help in understanding the complicated legal regime that applies to nonprofit chief executive compensation, our thanks go to Celia Roady and Greg Needles of Morgan, Lewis & Bockius. Without Celia's advice and editing skills, and Greg's expertise on deferred compensation, we never would have been able to complete the legal sections of the book.

Thanks are also due to our staff at Quatt Associates, in particular to Alex Rabinovich for his meticulous review and editing of multiple drafts, and to both Alex and Chris Potter for their research assistance.

To everyone who helped us, your assistance was invaluable; any remaining faults are ours.

Introduction

Hiring, compensating, and retaining the chief executive are some of the most important functions of a nonprofit organization's board. While the board is ultimately responsible for the organization's mission and strategy, the chief executive is the executor — and very often the main architect — of that strategy. The chief executive is also responsible for the day-to-day leadership of the organization and for its effective management.

Recruiting the best possible chief executive often depends on offering the right compensation plan. An effective compensation plan also enables a board to retain a good chief executive by providing appropriate signals about performance and rewards for effective leadership of the organization. In developing the compensation plan, the board must execute a careful balancing act. On the one hand, it must offer a strong salary and benefits package in order to both attract the best possible candidates for the chief executive position, and to keep that person in office if desired; on the other hand, it must not offer a compensation package that seems out of line with the organization's mission or with the overall culture of the nonprofit sector, whose work is regarded, both within and outside the sector, as properly mission oriented rather than profit oriented.

To complicate matters, the environment in which boards must make decisions about chief executive compensation has become more difficult. Outside scrutiny of nonprofit salaries has increased; both the media and the Internal Revenue Service (IRS) are paying much closer attention than they have in the past to nonprofit, and especially chief executive, compensation. In June 2004, the IRS announced that it was stepping up scrutiny of nonprofit salaries and hiring 73 new auditors to review nonprofit pay for compliance with IRS regulations; the agency's initial targets were organizations where an executive's compensation totaled more than $1 million a year.[1] State regulators, too, are cracking down on potentially excessive chief executive compensation; state attorneys general are bringing lawsuits that result in judgments ordering chief executives to repay millions of dollars in excess compensation. California's adoption of the California Nonprofit Integrity Act of 2004, which took effect in January 2005, *requires* the boards of charitable organizations with revenues of at least $2 million to review and approve the chief executive's compensation package to ensure its reasonableness. More and more state legislations are on the road to tightening regulation of the internal practices of nonprofits — with compensation becoming increasingly important.

As a consequence of this scrutiny, many large nonprofits have made commendable progress in changing their compensation plans and increasing the transparency of their processes for setting compensation and reviewing chief executive performance on a regular basis. However, many are still struggling to overcome the negative publicity and the resulting drop in public support that have come from accusations of impropriety. Although legal actions have primarily been brought against large

---

1. Elizabeth Schwinn. "Big Nonprofit Salaries Face Government Scrutiny." *Chronicle of Philanthropy*, June 24, 2004; Joann Lublin. "Compensation at Nonprofits is Scrutinized Amid Lawsuits." *Wall Street Journal* Online, June 1, 2004 (http://www.careerjournal.com/salaryhiring/industries/nonprofits /20040601-lublin.html).

nonprofits, investigative reporting has raised questions about the accountability of nonprofits of all sizes, and the credibility of the entire sector has been damaged.

Perhaps not coincidentally, the increased scrutiny from the government, the press, and the public comes at a time when compensation practices at many nonprofits increasingly resemble those in the for-profit sector. Salaries at many nonprofits have been rising,[2] and salaries at some large nonprofits have reached levels formerly associated only with the for-profit marketplace. In addition, some nonprofits have introduced compensation features such as bonuses, incentives, and deferred compensation that were formerly seen almost exclusively among for-profit corporations.

The IRS has recognized that untraditional forms of compensation, such as bonuses and incentives, can contribute to stronger and more successful nonprofit organizations. Estimates of the percentage of nonprofits with chief executive bonus or incentive programs vary: A 2004 Quatt Associates survey of large nonprofit organizations showed that 46.2 percent offered such programs, while the 2002 Buck Consultants *Not-For-Profit Compensation and Benefits Survey* found that only 39.1 percent did, and the Mercer *2004 Executive Compensation Survey* found that only 24.1 percent did. The median bonus was 22 percent in the Quatt Associates survey and 15 percent in the Buck survey.[3]

Of course, few nonprofit organizations have the luxury of offering excessive compensation to any of their staff members; the challenge that many smaller organizations face is not to control unreasonably high salaries, but to find enough money to pay reasonable salaries at all. This all-too-common financial challenge is one of the reasons that chief executive compensation in the nonprofit sector, like sector salaries in general, remains below the levels found in the for-profit world. In addition, nonprofits cannot offer some of the more lucrative features found in for-profit compensation, such as equity, and deferred compensation in the nonprofit sector is subject to stricter rules than it is in the for-profit world.

However, perhaps the most significant factor differentiating compensation for chief executives in the nonprofit sector from that of their counterparts in for-profit businesses is public expectation. The public rightly believes that a nonprofit organization has a responsibility to channel most of the money it receives from donors toward the fulfillment of its mission, not to staff compensation. Many members of the public also believe that staff at nonprofits should be willing to receive lower salaries than staff members in comparable positions in for-profit businesses do, because the nonprofit staff person is dedicated to the organization's mission.[4] These expectations create a value system in which an apparently generous, and perhaps appropriate, salary is seen to imply a lack of dedication to the organization and its mission, and compensation practices that are common in the for-profit sector, such as pay for performance and bonuses, are perceived as unethical.

---

2. Elizabeth Schwinn and Ian Wilhelm. "Nonprofit CEOs See Salaries Rise." *Chronicle of Philanthropy*, October 2, 2003; Ben Gose. "Executive Pay Rises Modestly." *Chronicle of Philanthropy*, October 14, 2004.

3. Buck Consultants. *2002 Not-For-Profit Compensation and Benefits Survey*. p. 66; Mercer. *2004 Executive Compensation Survey*. p. 100.000.112; Quatt Associates. *2004 Not-for-Profit Compensation Survey*. p. 8.

4. Sarah Z. Sleeper. "Sizing Up San Diego's Nonprofit CEO Pay." *San Diego Metropolitan*, June 2004 (http://www.sandiegometro.com/2004/jun/nonprofits.php).

Nonprofit boards must be prepared to work with, and within, the constraints imposed by this publicly held value system. They must also recognize that the same value system may be an integral part of their nonprofit's internal culture as well. When this is the case, board members and staff alike may object to the use of market comparisons for making salary determinations and to the provision of benefits and perquisites for the chief executive. They may even resist giving the chief executive more than a token annual salary increase.

Boards need to be aware, however, that unrealistic expectations about executive compensation can be detrimental to a nonprofit organization. The chief executive is a nonprofit's single most important employee. Failure to pay a market-based salary, however noble the motivation for doing so, can cause a nonprofit to lose a strong chief executive or find it almost impossible to recruit an effective one, harming the organization's success and its ability to fulfill its mission. Below-market chief executive compensation can also act as a cap on the pay of other senior staff, leading to further losses in effectiveness as key employees are recruited away.

Board members should therefore consider very carefully the potential costs of under-paying their organization's chief executive. For organizations that can afford them and are prepared to justify them, market-based salaries and innovative compensation practices can help recruit and retain skilled and experienced leaders. For organizations that are facing budget constraints, it may make sense to economize in other areas rather than risk the loss of an effective organizational leader. Of course, each nonprofit must decide for itself what mix of compensation features makes the most sense for its individual circumstances.

A nonprofit organization's board can most effectively meet public expectations and justify its decisions regarding chief executive compensation when it approaches compensation as a strategic decision. Because the board's principal duty in setting chief executive pay is to ensure that the compensation package supports organizational success, that package must be considered as an integral part of overall organizational strategy and planning. By ensuring that the chief executive's compensation will contribute to the realization of the organization's mission and objectives, the board provides a rationale for its decisions that will stand up to public scrutiny.

This book is intended as a practical guide for nonprofit boards in determining chief executive compensation — both in the face of hiring a new chief executive and to revisit the compensation strategy on a regular basis, regardless of staff changes. It is designed to serve as a reference tool and as a step-by-step guide that any board can use to establish an effective compensation structure within the context of the organization's mission, history, goals, and marketplace. It seeks to provide information and guidelines that will be useful to nonprofits of all sizes, while recognizing that small, medium-sized, and large nonprofits have differing needs and circumstances. Above all, it aims to help nonprofits of all types to increase the transparency and integrity of their chief executive compensation practices as part of their stewardship of the public trust.

1.
Understanding the Board's Role in Setting Chief Executive Compensation

In one sense the board's role in setting chief executive compensation is simple: The board is responsible for recruiting and hiring the chief executive, overseeing the chief executive's performance, and, if necessary, terminating the chief executive's contract. Setting the chief executive's compensation is part of this responsibility.

However, the board's responsibility is more complex than this simple statement would suggest. The board must not only create a compensation plan that will be an effective tool both in recruitment and in performance evaluation, it must also set compensation in light of its responsibilities to the organization.

- **Mission responsibility:** The board ensures that the organization will achieve its mission through its oversight of the organization's long-term strategy and objectives. This means that the board must hire a chief executive who will be effective in implementing that strategy and therefore in leading the organization toward mission achievement. The compensation structure is an essential element of the board's ability to attract such a chief executive. However, the compensation structure itself must reinforce the organization's strategy. A strategic compensation structure will reward success and send the appropriate signals if performance falls short; it will work best if it is part of an overall performance management plan tied to board-approved annual and long-term goals and objectives.

- **Fiduciary responsibility:** The board has a duty to maintain the organization's financial integrity. Chief executive compensation must therefore be affordable within the organization's overall budget, so that it does not become a drain on the organization's resources. However, paying too low a salary can result in difficulty in recruiting and retaining an effective leader, to the detriment of managerial decision making and ultimately of the organization's overall effectiveness. The board must strike a balance that allows it to hire the best possible chief executive without breaking the bank. As Dennis Pointer and James Orlikoff suggest, "CEO compensation should be viewed as an important investment in the organization's future, not an expense. Value added to the organization by the CEO should be a huge multiple of total compensation. Your board must be prudent, but not penny wise and pound foolish."[5]

- **Legal responsibility:** The board must ensure that the organization complies with legal standards and meets the test of public and stakeholder scrutiny. This is not just an ethical responsibility; by federal law, board members are personally responsible and subject to legal penalties if chief executive compensation is found to be excessive.

---

5. D. D. Pointer and J. E. Orlikoff. *The High-Performance Board*. San Francisco: Jossey-Bass, 2002. p. 37.

In order to fulfill its duties in these three areas responsibly, the board needs to establish a procedure for determining a chief executive compensation level and plan before it begins the recruiting and hiring process or in revisiting and revising the compensation package for the current chief executive. This procedure should consist of a series of well-thought-out steps that are formally outlined in writing for future reference. The board should begin by determining its internal structure for overseeing chief executive compensation. That structure may take one of three forms.

1. Where the board is too large and unwieldy to manage the compensation process as a group, it may delegate oversight of chief executive compensation to a special compensation committee or task force. A smaller committee can devote its attention as needed to the often-detailed process of managing compensation matters; over time, committee members can also develop experience and a certain degree of expertise in this area. In many organizations, the compensation committee also reviews the staff compensation levels suggested by the chief executive, and it can take the lead in setting annual performance objectives and reviewing chief executive and organizational performance.

2. If the board wishes to delegate compensation matters to a smaller committee but does not have the desire or personnel to form a separate compensation committee, chief executive and staff compensation may be handled by the board's executive committee. In the university community, for example, a 2003 Quatt Associates survey found that 38.7 percent had compensation committees; among those without compensation committees, 79.3 percent delegated chief executive compensation matters to the executive committee, and only 20.7 percent assigned them to the full board.[6]

3. In small and medium-sized nonprofits and in nonprofits with small boards, oversight of chief executive compensation may be handled by the board as a whole. (*For the sake of simplicity, the remainder of this book will refer to the* **compensation committee** *as taking the lead in managing the chief executive compensation process. This implies no judgment as to the appropriate structure for any particular board and will apply to any group that is managing the process.*)

Review of chief executive compensation by the full board (regardless of whether or not a separate committee is responsible for the major responsibilities involving compensation) is not just good practice; it is vital because chief executive compensation is public domain information. Each board member should therefore understand and be able to justify the full board's compensation decision, as well as the board's overall process for setting and reviewing chief executive compensation, including the respective roles of the full board and any smaller committee(s).

As board members seek to determine which internal structure will work best for their organization, the answers to these questions may provide guidance:

1. Is our board small and efficient enough to handle chief executive compensation matters as a group? Would the two-step process of committee work followed by full board review be more cumbersome for us than full board discussion of these matters?

---

6. Quatt Associates. *2003 Compensation and Benefits Survey* sponsored by the Association of Governing Boards of Universities and Colleges. p. 12.

2. Do we currently have access to the expertise we need to make informed decisions, either among our board members or with outside resources (legal advisor, compensation consultant, accountant, board members from other organizations)?

3. Are we more comfortable with assigning oversight of chief executive compensation to our executive committee, or to a separate compensation committee?

4. Do we have board members who are willing and able to take the lead as part of a compensation committee, executive committee, or special task force?

Once the board has decided on its internal structure, it then needs to consider and approve the subsequent steps in its overall procedure for establishing chief executive compensation. On each of the following tasks a committee or task force may take the lead rather than the full board. This includes the review of compensation for intermediate sanctions purposes. The committee must exclude any person with a conflict of interest.

CHECKLIST FOR ESTABLISHING A CHIEF EXECUTIVE COMPENSATION PLAN

___ Ensure that the chief executive compensation plan supports the organization's mission, goals, and strategy.

___ Establish the chief executive job description and profile (and title, if necessary).

___ Develop the organization's compensation philosophy.

___ Understand the marketplace; acquire and analyze appropriate market data on compensation practices in comparable organizations.

___ Ensure that the compensation level and structure will meet legal requirements; establish a process for documenting the chief executive compensation decision and ensure that the process is followed; retain legal counsel if necessary.

___ Review compensation for purposes of stakeholder and public scrutiny.

___ Establish the compensation level and plan.

___ Establish an ongoing process for reviewing chief executive compensation and job performance. The process should include setting annual and long-term goals, conducting annual performance reviews, and adjusting compensation each year based on market and performance.

___ Identify negotiation points with respect to the chief executive contract.

Although these tasks are outlined in a sequential way here and in the chapters that follow, the overall process is not a linear one. The compensation committee will need to start with some sense of the possibilities that its mission, goals, and budget dictate for salary, benefits, and other compensation, and use those as reference points throughout the study and research process. Completion of each of the tasks outlined above will clarify that initial picture and enable the committee to develop a realistic and effective compensation plan.

The compensation committee must also start with accurate and detailed information about the current compensation packages for the chief executive and other senior staff. Particularly in situations where the full board has not previously been involved in setting chief executive compensation, full disclosure of the base pay level, the types and amounts of bonuses and other benefits, and the rationale for each is crucial. Organization staff must provide this information when the board requests it; typically, the board establishes a formal reporting mechanism through which the staff provides compensation information to the board chair, the chair of the compensation committee, or the compensation committee as a whole.

After the board has done this preparatory work, it should draft a formal document outlining the compensation process. This is useful for legal reasons, and from a practical standpoint it can also serve as a more detailed checklist for the board or compensation committee. The first part of the document should outline the relationship between chief executive compensation and the organization's mission. These details will be discussed further in subsequent chapters.

2.
Aligning Compensation with Organizational Mission, Goals, and Culture

Once the board has identified its mechanism for overseeing chief executive compensation, the next step is to review the organization's mission, strategy, and performance goals. Understanding these will help the compensation committee determine the skills and qualities wanted in a chief executive, the appropriate level of chief executive compensation, the structure of the compensation plan, and the process for regular review of performance and compensation level. The organization's culture — the expectations, habits, and beliefs of the organization's key supporters and stakeholders — is another key determinant that can guide the compensation committee in establishing the chief executive compensation structure.

Review of the organization's mission and strategy is a task for the full board. The board's goal should be to put on paper its current priorities for the organization and its key objectives for the next three to five years. This list should include major priorities and the objectives associated with them, along with a brief outline of the action steps that will be necessary to accomplish each objective. The list should be limited to four or five major priorities; targeting more than five priorities makes the goal-setting process unwieldy and can dilute the focus of the organization.

The strategic review need not be time consuming, but a formal process, even a brief one, is helpful. A day or half-day spent thinking through strategic objectives and putting them on paper is highly recommended; a clear and focused set of priorities and objectives will help the compensation committee see what qualities, skills, and experience will be most important in the new chief executive. (Please see page 80 of Suggested Resources for a helpful tool in the strategic planning process.)

MEASURING PERFORMANCE: THE BALANCED SCORECARD APPROACH

If a strategic plan is already in place, the board should review it to ensure that it will continue to be appropriate through the search process and under a new chief executive. If no plan is in place, or if a rethinking is in order, one effective option for the board is the balanced scorecard approach, which allows an organization to think about performance in terms of multiple categories. Robert Kaplan and David Norton of the Harvard Business School introduced the balanced scorecard in the early 1990s in recognition of the fact that financial performance measures alone do not necessarily ensure long-term organizational health.[7] The balanced scorecard organizes strategy and mission objectives into four primary areas of performance: customer (best understood as *mission* in the nonprofit context), financial, internal, and innovation and learning.

---

7. Robert S. Kaplan and David P. Norton. *Translating Strategy into Action: The Balanced Scorecard.* Boston: Harvard Business School Press, 1996.

Many organizations and management advisors have found the balanced scorecard approach valuable. It works especially well in the nonprofit sector, where financial measures do not define organizational success because the organizational mission is not about making a profit. Using the balanced scorecard approach, a nonprofit organization might ask the following series of questions to define its objectives in the four performance areas:

Mission: How well is the organization serving its clients or target population? How can the organization serve its clients or target population more effectively? How is the organization managing its relations with its stakeholders? How can the organi-zation ensure that key stakeholders — members, donors, and others — remain committed to the organization and increase their support?

Financial: What is the organization's current financial picture? How much and in what ways must the financial picture change in order for the organization to achieve its overall mission and its nonfinancial objectives?

Internal: What is the current structure of internal operations? How does the organization need to improve its internal operations in order to better achieve its mission?

Innovation and learning: What must the organization do to ensure that it can continue to be viable? In what ways has the organization been growing, and in what ways has it been stagnant or shrinking? In what areas is growth desirable, and what must the organization do to initiate and sustain that growth?

UNDERSTANDING ORGANIZATIONAL CULTURE

Reflection on the organization's culture is another important aspect of the initial review of strategy and objectives. The organization's mission, its founders' vision, and the attitudes of its staff and supporters all may contribute to an understanding of the appropriate compensation level and plan for its chief executive. Organizations with a religious background, for example, may be uncomfortable with fully market-based levels of compensation. Charities can sometimes be uncomfortable with including an incentive element in the compensation package. Numerous nonprofits also pride themselves on being informal and nonbureaucratic; such organizations may resist a highly structured compensation and performance review process. A compensation committee that tries to impose a compensation level or plan inconsistent with the organizational culture could find itself alienating key staff members and outside stakeholders.

In order to understand the organization's culture, the compensation committee can interview key staff members and long-serving board members. The existing staff compensation system may also be an indicator of the organizational culture. If salaries are generally low compared to the market, this may reflect a service ethos that might be at odds with a more aggressive chief executive compensation package. Of course, low salaries may also reflect an organization's financial situation, or simple organizational inertia. The absence of a coherent compensation system may also reflect the conscious choice of an informal operating style.

When the review of organizational priorities and culture is complete, the compensation committee should then consider the implications for the chief executive position. In doing so, the committee may want to use the following questions as a guide:

- What qualities are desirable in the chief executive? Does the organization need someone who is primarily a manager? A fundraiser? A mission specialist?

- How much and what kind of experience is required in the chief executive?

- What is the marketplace for the chief executive? Might a new chief executive be recruited from within the organization? From other nonprofits? From the for-profit sector? Should recruitment take place locally, regionally, or nationally? Where might the chief executive go for his or her next position?

- What is the financial situation of the organization? How is the level of compensation that can be offered affected by the organization's financial constraints?

- What constraints does the organizational culture put on chief executive compensation in terms of level of compensation and acceptable compensation structure?

The following three examples illustrate different ways in which a board's review of organizational priorities and culture can affect compensation decisions.

Organization A *is a nationwide membership association. It has a strong program that combines member benefits such as reduced-price insurance and travel opportunities with quality professional development opportunities for members, and as a result has built a steady and loyal membership. With the retirement of the longtime chief executive, A's board has a chance to evaluate the association's situation. As a result, the board identifies a major lack in the association's operations: It is not serving its members as well as it could because it has no strategic plan for advocacy at the federal or state level. It is not playing the role it should in identifying and responding to political issues that affect its members.*

A's board sets two primary priorities, with associated objectives:

1. *A mission priority, to serve its members more effectively by adding advocacy to its activities; objectives include developing an advocacy policy within a year, and identifying existing connections in national and state political circles within six months.*

2. *A learning priority, to develop board and staff understanding of the workings of advocacy; objectives include hiring a consultant to provide guidance in the development of this new area.*

A's compensation committee then connects these new priorities with its chief executive search process. Because existing programs are already efficiently managed by lower-level staff, and because development of the advocacy aspect will be a major leap for the organization, committee members agree that the new chief executive should be someone who can spearhead the advocacy effort. This in turn has implications for the kinds of connections and background that the committee will seek in the new chief executive, and therefore for the compensation level that will be required to attract the right person.

Organization B *is a social service agency that serves impoverished citizens in a major city. It has grown rapidly over the past 10 years and has become recognized as a leading contributor to the well-being of the city's needy. However, over the past year, whistle-blowing by two staff members and an inquiry by the board have led to charges that the* executive director and another staff member embezzled significant amounts from the organization. As a result of the ensuing negative publicity, B has lost a significant portion of its donor base as well as much of its credibility with the public.

The board realizes that its first priority must be to downsize the organization so that it can continue to function with reduced levels of financial support and regain some measure of public trust. For the new executive director, the board's search committee thus seeks someone who can manage a staff and facility restructuring, oversee a limited public relations program, and find ways to reduce administrative costs — and one who is willing to accept a relatively low level of compensation while doing so.

Organization C is a private secondary school that has a national reputation for the quality of the education it provides. It has achieved that reputation and its related success in sending its graduates to prestigious universities under its longtime head, who is beloved and respected by students, parents, staff, and board members alike. As the time nears for the head to retire, the board wrestles over what to do. For many board members, strategic planning and examination of the school's mission are useless exercises; the mission is just fine the way it is, and the only strategy they need is one for finding a successor who is an exact replica of the current head, only 20 years younger. The attitude of these board members is shared by a significant portion of the staff.

However, other board members realize that the school cannot possibly expect to recruit someone with the current head's profile for one major reason: The school, though it enrolls students from a variety of religious backgrounds, was founded by a specific religious tradition, and its head has always been a member of the clergy. As a result, the head's compensation has always been set in accordance with clergy salary guidelines (that is, it has been significantly lower than the salaries of nonclergy in comparable positions), and no health or retirement benefits have been needed because these have been covered by the clergy association. Due to a precipitous decline in the number of ordinations in recent years, however, the board is facing the likelihood that it will have to hire a layperson as the new head of school. The board will need to determine how it can provide a competitive compensation package for its new head — but first it will have to work through the organizational culture issues inherent in the situation.

These examples portray some of the ways that the larger organizational picture can affect a compensation committee's decisions. Once it has reviewed the organization's priorities, goals, and culture, and ascertained their implications for the chief executive's profile and compensation, the compensation committee can address the next steps in the process: developing a title, job description, and profile for the position; creating a compensation philosophy that formally articulates the principles that will guide the board in setting compensation; and determining the marketplace for the position.

3.
Outlining the Title, Job Description, and Profile

Having defined the organization's priorities and objectives, and assessed the chief executive's role in meeting those objectives, the compensation committee next needs to classify the chief executive position in a formal way. It should do so by drafting a new job description or updating an existing one. The job description outlines the duties of the chief executive and the most important responsibilities of the position; outlining these duties and responsibilities will help the compensation committee to define performance expectations and the qualities desired in a candidate for the position, as well as perform a necessary review of the current chief executive (especially if that person has been in office for some time) on a regular basis.

In some cases the compensation committee may also need to designate the chief executive's title. A nonprofit chief executive may be called executive director, director, administrator, president, or chief executive officer (CEO). There is no bright-line distinction among these titles, but the ways in which they are customarily used can provide a guideline.

- In community service organizations and membership organizations such as associations, the chief executive is most often called *executive director*. This title conveys the sense that the person is leading the staff in carrying out a service mission.

- In cultural and arts institutions, the chief executive is often called *director*, as in the director of a museum. However, where confusion with another use of the term *director* may occur (as in a theater), *executive director* may be used instead.

- In education, the chief executive of a university or college is the *president*, and the chief executive of a private elementary or secondary school is the *head of school* or *principal*. These titles differentiate the chief executive, whose work focuses on overall leadership and external relations, from the *dean*, whose work focuses more on internal matters.

- In health care, the chief executive of a hospital is often called *administrator*, a title that reflects the managerial and fiscal responsibilities of the position.

- In other types of nonprofits, especially larger ones, *president* and *CEO* are commonly used to designate the chief executive. These titles, especially when combined, convey a sense of the person's overall leadership role in the organization.

In fact, more and more nonprofits are designating their chief executives as *president* or *CEO*. As Richard Chait, William Ryan, and Barbara Taylor point out, this reflects changes both in the chief executive and in stakeholder expectations:

> Yesterday's naïve nonprofit administrator or executive director has become today's sophisticated president or CEO, titles that betray changes in the stature, perception, and professionalism of the positions. ... Many executives have earned graduate degrees in nonprofit management. ... More important, nonprofit executives have acquired what formal

education alone cannot confer: standing as organizational leaders (a status often underscored by the compensation package). As a result, trustees, employees, clients, and donors expect far more of nonprofit CEOs today than a genial personality, moral probity, managerial acumen, and a passionate commitment to the organization's social mission. Stakeholders, in a word, expect *leadership*.[8]

In the final analysis, however, the choice of title will depend on the preferences of the board, the history and culture of the organization, and the preferences of the person holding or seeking the position.

The title and job description should reflect the strategic objectives that the organization hopes to achieve in hiring the chief executive. One organization might emphasize fundraising over internal management; for another, external representation might be especially important. The drafting of the job description therefore provides the first opportunity to establish performance expectations that are in line with the organization's priorities and objectives.

MAJOR ELEMENTS OF A CHIEF EXECUTIVE JOB DESCRIPTION

It is a mistake simply to take an off-the-shelf chief executive job description and use it without review. While the elements of a chief executive job description are likely to be similar across organizations, the emphasis placed on those elements will not be. Nor should an organization simply reuse an existing job description. Before hiring a new chief executive, the organization should carefully review any existing job description to make sure it still accurately reflects the organization's priorities and goals. Are the responsibilities clearly defined and measurable? Have changes in the organization's mission or changes in the environment created new challenges and responsibilities for the executive? Having a valid, updated job description will allow the board to measure its executive position against those of other organizations when conducting the necessary research. The board should never forget that a good job description for the chief executive will clearly define the chief executive's role with respect to the role of the board.

As it begins to develop its chief executive job description, the compensation committee can guide itself through the use of the following questionnaire.

8. Richard P. Chait, William P. Ryan, and Barbara E. Taylor. *Governance as Leadership*. New York: John Wiley & Sons, 2005. pp. 2–3.

QUESTIONNAIRE 1: WHAT ARE THE MAJOR RESPONSIBILITIES OF THE CHIEF EXECUTIVE IN MEETING ORGANIZATIONAL CHALLENGES?

1. What are the most significant external challenges that the organization will face in the next three to five years? Internal challenges?

2. What will the chief executive need to do to meet those challenges successfully?

3. Prioritize the activities below in terms of relative importance for the chief executive's allotment of time. For each area, describe the results that you expect the chief executive to achieve.

   _____ Vision and planning for the future of the organization

   _____ Leadership and internal management of the organization; providing a clear direction for staff

   _____ Relations with supporters, stakeholders, donors

   _____ Advocacy/representing the organization to the public

   _____ Fundraising and development

   _____ Financial health of the organization

   _____ Carrying out the organization's mission

   _____ Working with the board in advising, board development, and carrying out the board's direction

   _____ Other: _____

4. Given your answer to #3, what will be the two or three most important responsibilities of the chief executive?

Using the answers to each element of the questionnaire, the compensation committee can develop a job description for the chief executive position. The description may be built on the elements in the following list, sequenced in accordance with their relative priority for the specific organization.

Mission role: State the organization's mission and goals, and outline the specific steps that the chief executive will take to achieve them.

Leadership role: State the role that the chief executive will play in relationship to the board, including advising the board and assisting with board development; conducting strategic planning and implementing strategic plans; and acting as the organization's chief visionary, positioning the organization for future effectiveness.

Public role: Outline the ways in which the chief executive will represent the organization and lead outreach to the public and to the organization's stakeholders.

Administrative role: Describe the chief executive's role in overseeing the design, promotion, and delivery of the programs, products, and services of the organization.

Fiscal role: Outline the chief executive's role in ensuring the financial integrity and health of the organization, including managing organizational resources, leading the annual and multiyear budget process, overseeing financial management and effective cost control, and ensuring compliance with government and internal financial controls and requirements.

Compliance role: State what the chief executive will do to ensure the organization's compliance with legal requirements, including preserving nonprofit status and complying with all reporting and other aspects of federal, state, and local law.

Human resources role: Describe the ways in which the chief executive will build and maintain human capital, including recruiting and retaining quality staff, leading the organization in improving the skills of staff members, and recruiting and retaining an effective corps of volunteers.

Development role: Outline the chief executive's role in fundraising, including setting goals, organizing the fundraising effort, and, where appropriate, acting as the organization's chief fundraiser.

Using the title and job description, as well as the results of its review of the organization's priorities, goals, and culture, the compensation committee can develop a profile of the ideal chief executive for the organization. The profile will list the characteristics of the chief executive in terms of knowledge, skills, capabilities, experience, background, and personal values. The following questionnaire may be helpful in guiding the committee as it identifies these characteristics. Committees that have carried out a careful review thus far will find significant overlap in the answers to the first two questions.

The great danger in this process is that the compensation committee will come out of it with a profile that only a divine being could match. To avoid the "in spare time, walks on water" syndrome, committee members should limit their consideration to the two or three most important elements in the job description and the two greatest challenges that lie ahead, and should identify only two or three attributes in response to each of the other questions. Doing so will help committee members separate essential characteristics from those they can get along without. They will then be ready to develop the organization's compensation philosophy.

QUESTIONNAIRE 2: WHAT CHARACTERISTICS ARE MOST IMPORTANT FOR CONSIDERATION IN FINDING THE RIGHT CHIEF EXECUTIVE?

1. Consider the two or three most important elements in the chief executive job description. What are the most critical characteristics (skills, capabilities, experience, and background) that the chief executive will need to have to perform those tasks successfully?

2. Consider the two greatest challenges that lie ahead for the organization. What are the most critical characteristics (skills, capabilities, experience, and background) that the chief executive will need to have to meet those challenges successfully?

3. What advantages would an internal candidate have in this position? An external candidate? Why?

4. What are the critical personal values that the chief executive of this organization must have to be successful?

5. What personal attributes or skill and knowledge gaps might prevent the chief executive from being effective in the position?

6. What characteristics would you not want to see in the next chief executive?

7. Which attributes of the current chief executive contribute most to his or her success in the position? Why?

8. Will these same attributes be equally critical for the next chief executive? What might change?

4.
Developing a Compensation Philosophy

An organization's compensation philosophy lays out the values, principles, and guidelines for the organization's overall compensation structure and supporting systems. Developing a compensation philosophy ensures that the board explicitly considers the most critical issues involved in defining appropriate compensation. When an organization reaches consensus on its compensation philosophy before developing a new compensation structure or introducing new compensation-related systems, it is far less likely to encounter problems with perceived inequities and disparities later on. A well-thought-out compensation philosophy will provide ongoing guidance to the organization on staff compensation in general, as well as supporting the immediate goal of developing a chief executive compensation plan.

A good compensation philosophy is based on an understanding of the organization's strategic goals and culture. In terms of process, a draft compensation philosophy is probably best developed by a small task force that is part of the compensation committee or the full board; if a consultant has been retained to advise on the chief executive search, he or she can help in drafting the philosophy. The draft should then be presented to the full board for approval. The task force should work with the current chief executive on the compensation philosophy; in the absence of a current chief executive, the task force should consult senior staff members who understand the organization's history, culture, and expectations.

The compensation philosophy should cover the following:

1. The objectives of the compensation plan. Examples:

   • To reflect and promote the organization's mission and values

   • To support the organization's strategies for carrying out its mission

   • To enable the organization to attract, motivate, and retain the executive talent needed to carry out its mission

2. The appropriate marketplace for the organization and the desired position in the marketplace. Examples:

   • The marketplace consists of organizations of similar size and general mission that are located in the same geographic area or areas similar to it. For example, the marketplace could be arts organizations with budgets between $10 million and $50 million located in major metropolitan areas.

   • The organization will pay base salaries at the median (or first quartile, or third quartile) of the marketplace.

   • The organization will pay total cash for exceptional performance at no greater than the 50th (or 25th, or 75th) percentile of the marketplace.

3. How compensation will be linked to performance and other factors. Examples:

- Compensation will reward outstanding performers and provide appropriate signals to staff members needing improvement.

- Compensation will be linked to an annual performance management process, with individual and organizational goals.

- Compensation adjustments will be based on achievement of those goals.

4. Whether the organization is open to incorporating bonus, incentive, or other pay-at-risk elements in the compensation system. Example:

- The compensation structure will (will not) include incentive and other reward systems where appropriate to the organization's marketplace.

5. The degree of formality and structure with which the organization is comfortable. Example:

- The compensation structure will be based on a single set of salary ranges; or salaries appropriate to professional areas/positions will be individually matched to the marketplace.

6. Other characteristics of the compensation system. Example:

- The system will be clearly and regularly communicated to staff.

- The structure will take into account community standards and the organization's role in the community (such as its faith-based origins).

In the sample compensation philosophy that follows (please refer to page 16), *compensation system* refers to the overall system for managing pay and benefits, assessing performance, and integrating compensation with organizational strategy and objectives. *Compensation structure* refers to the formal mechanisms that are part of the compensation system, including the hierarchy of salaries and other benefits that apply to employees of the organization. The purpose of the philosophy is to articulate the principles that govern the structure and the elements that will be included in the system, not to specify the exact nature of these; for this reason, the philosophy does not describe the hierarchy of positions within the organization, the amounts of base pay and incentives, or the specific parameters for conducting performance evaluation.

With its chief executive profile and compensation philosophy in place, the compensation committee will be in a position to investigate the marketplace from which it will draw its pool of chief executive candidates.

SAMPLE COMPENSATION PHILOSOPHY

- The compensation structure and systems of our organization will support our mission, strategy, and values.

- We will pay for performance, skills and competencies, development and growth, and effective visible commitment to the organization.

- The compensation system will encourage recruitment, retention, and motivation of outstanding employees so that the organization can achieve its mission and objectives.

- The compensation system will reward truly outstanding performers and provide appropriate feedback to staff members who need improvement.

- Our compensation structure will be a mixture of base salary; performance-based "at risk" pay appropriate to the nonprofit marketplace; retirement and other benefits; and special recognition awards where merited by performance.

- A portion of each employee's pay will be tied to the achievement of organizational and individual objectives. Unusual individual achievement may also merit special financial awards.

- Our compensation system will include annual adjustments to pay ranges based on changes in the marketplace (subject to financial constraints). Adjustments to individual base pay will be based on job performance and growth in mastering job competencies. All adjustments to pay will be consistent with practice in the nonprofit marketplace.

- The compensation system will have a coherent structure based on pay practices consistent with our not-for-profit mission and status, but will recognize that parts of our organization are in different markets and that the compensation for each position must be based on the appropriate marketplace for that professional area.

- We will pay as close as possible to the median (midpoint) of the appropriate external marketplace, while recognizing that internal equity and financial constraints can justify some deviation from the market.

- The marketplace adequacy of the structure will be judged in terms of total compensation, including benefits; the total package will be competitive with the marketplace.

- The compensation structure will be linked to an effective performance management system with individual growth and development as well as professional achievement goals. The goals will be accompanied by effective benchmarks for measuring success.

- Executives and staff will receive regular and comprehensive training in the compensation system.

5.
Understanding the Marketplace

The compensation committee's next task is to understand the marketplace — with an emphasis on the nonprofit marketplace in general, and the specific marketplace for the organization. In some cases it may also be appropriate to understand aspects of the for-profit marketplace, especially for those nonprofits (health care organizations, for example) that may compete for talent with the for-profit sector.

For reasons of both law and custom, the nonprofit marketplace in general is more constrained in its pay practices than the for-profit market with which some board members may be more familiar. Even where there is some degree of for-profit competition for executive talent, nonprofit practices take precedence. The specific marketplace for the organization sets further limits — again both in terms of customary practice and legal requirements — on what a particular nonprofit can pay its chief executive and on the kind of compensation structure that is suitable for the organization.

Some organizations will choose to retain a compensation consultant to help analyze the organization's marketplace. A consultant's experience, understanding of the local market, and access to data sources can help a compensation committee understand its options. A set of guidelines for hiring a compensation consultant can be found in Appendix I on page 60.

Whether or not a consultant is retained, the board is ultimately responsible for the compensation decision, and therefore should have a basic understanding of the relevant marketplace. IRS regulations require the board to make a reasoned judgment on executive compensation; to meet the legal standard, the board must consider data that is sufficiently detailed and reflective of the organization's particular marketplace to allow such a reasoned judgment to be made (see Chapter 6 for further discussion of the rebuttable presumption of reasonableness for intermediate sanctions purposes). A board that already has some understanding of the relevant market will be in a better position to judge the suitability of the data with which it is presented.

THE NONPROFIT MARKETPLACE

As noted in the introduction, nonprofit salaries have risen over the last decade, and pay practices such as bonus and deferred compensation, formerly seen only in for-profit organizations, are now increasingly common in nonprofit organizations, though they remain a minority practice.[9] Nevertheless, pay in the nonprofit sector remains below that of the for-profit sector, especially at the top of the organization. Even chief executives who expect competitive pay do not generally expect that their nonprofit compensation will equal what they could earn in the for-profit world. Earning money is not the mission of nonprofits. Most nonprofit employees — and all

---

9. Surveys differ on the percentage of nonprofits that provide extra cash compensation to chief executives, from a low of 24 percent to a high of 56 percent (Elizabeth Schwinn, "Big Nonprofit Salaries Face Government Scrutiny," *Chronicle of Philanthropy*, June 24, 2004). Since all the surveys cited cover large and/or national nonprofits, the actual practice among all nonprofits is likely to be lower than the survey data suggest.

good nonprofit chief executives — get their deepest job satisfaction from helping their organizations achieve their missions.

Historically, the nonprofit sector has been particularly conservative in its approach to non-base pay (e.g., bonus or incentive) compensation. Before making extra cash compensation part of a chief executive compensation package, boards need to be sure that such an arrangement will be acceptable within their particular marketplace, as well as consistent with their organization's culture and expectations. This is partly for legal reasons, but it also serves to protect the organization's reputation with stake-holders, staff, and the public. The public expects that the compensation level at a given nonprofit will conform to practice in the nonprofit, not the for-profit, marketplace. Expectations for particular organizations may be even stronger — faith-based institutions, volunteer organizations, advocacy organizations, and others may all have compensation expectations shaped by their history, membership, or donor base.

From a legal perspective, IRS regulations provide a general limit on the total amount of compensation, and they also limit deferral options, both as to types of deferral vehicles and to the amount that can be deferred in particular vehicles. Also, because there is no equity available in a nonprofit organization, boards should be wary of any compensation arrangement that looks like the distribution of revenues.

THE ORGANIZATION'S SPECIFIC MARKETPLACE

While nonprofit status by itself places some constraints on chief executive compensation, it is the particular marketplace for an organization that principally determines what it can and must pay its chief executive. The IRS reasonableness standard provides a good definition of an organization's specific marketplace: "What would ordinarily be paid for like services by like enterprises under like circumstances."[10] When defining an organization's marketplace, compensation committee members should take the items in the following box (please refer to the next page) into account.

No single factor alone determines the marketplace. The goal should be to specify the marketplace in terms of all the relevant factors. Thus, to take one example, the market for the chief executive of a museum in New York City might be defined by the following factors:

- **Mission:** Preservation and display of, and public education concerning, artifacts

- **Recruitment sources:** Museums, art galleries, university art departments

- **Organization size:** Budget between $15 and $25 million; approximately 200 employees

- **Organization scope:** National (that is, recruits nationally for the chief executive)

- **Organization location:** New York City

- **Specific requirements:** Must hold a Ph.D. in art history

- **Service/experience:** Must have served in senior positions for at least 10 years

This organization would then look for market data on organizations as close as possible to this description.

---

10. Internal Revenue Service. *Instructions for Form 990 and Form 990 E-Z 2003.* p. 12.

FACTORS TO CONSIDER WHEN DEFINING YOUR ORGANIZATION'S MARKETPLACE

- *The organization's mission:* Committee members should first consider which organizations are doing the same or similar types of work.

- *Organization size:* Organizations should compare themselves to others within a reasonable size range as measured in terms of budget and number of staff. Standard surveys usually organize their data into budget and staff size groupings, for example, below $2.5 million, $2.5 to $5 million, $5 million to $10 million, and so on. Endowment size (for those organizations that have endowments, such as foundations) is another measure of organization size.

- *Organization scope:* Does the organization work entirely at the local level? Is it statewide? Regional? National? International?

- *Organization location:* Where is the organization based? An organization may be national in scope, and hence recruit in a national marketplace, but be located in a place with an unusually high or low cost of living that should be reflected in the salary. For example, compensation in New York City is generally above national market levels because of the extremely high cost of living in Manhattan.

- *The specific requirements for the position:* The strategic analysis and job description should determine the specific and special needs for the position. Special technical skills can be a factor in determining the appropriate marketplace — for example, the chief executive must be an M.D. or a lawyer, or have experience in media or information technology.

- *Length of service and experience:* In determining the appropriate marketplace for a serving chief executive, it is appropriate to look at organizations whose chief executives have comparable length of service and experience.

- *Chief executive recruitment sources:* Types of organizations from which a chief executive might be recruited, or to which he or she might go, can be included even if the missions of such organizations are somewhat different. The goal is to establish the market for the chief executive's services. A word of caution here: Although understanding recruitment sources can help in setting compensation, it does not determine compensation, especially when the candidates are being recruited from the for-profit sector. The fact that an executive from the for-profit sector is considered a viable candidate for a nonprofit position does not necessarily define the marketplace. Pay must always meet nonprofit market standards.

SOURCES OF MARKET INFORMATION

Market information comes from three sources: publicly available IRS data, publicly available surveys, and specially commissioned surveys. As a rule of thumb, a compensation committee should obtain data from at least three independent sources, including IRS 990 data and two or more relevant public surveys.

IRS 990 Data

Most nonprofit organizations with annual budgets over $25,000 are required to file an IRS Form 990 or 990E-Z every year (see the instructions to the most recent IRS Form 990 for exceptions). Organizations must list the names, addresses, and salaries of their five highest-paid employees, including contributions to their employee benefit plans, their expense accounts, and other allowances. 990 data is available to the public; the 990s from the past three years must be made available to anyone who visits a nonprofit and asks for them, and nonprofits have 30 days to send out a photocopy if one is requested in writing. If an organization posts its 990 on the World Wide Web, however, it is exempt from the other disclosure requirements. The nonprofit organization, Guidestar (www.guidestar.org), posts 990 data for approximately 390,000 individual organizations on the Web; details of Guidestar's IRS 990-based database are available for a fee. Other organizations, including the *Chronicle of Philanthropy*, also publish selected 990 data from time to time.

Form 990 filings are therefore an obvious and easily obtained source of compensation data on particular comparable organizations. A compensation committee can develop a list of organizations it sees as comparable and obtain information on their chief executive compensation with little effort or expense. However, several aspects of the 990 data should be kept in mind:

- Organizations report only total cash, deferred compensation, and fringe benefits. Thus, while the data are useful for understanding the marketplace for total cash compensation, they are not as helpful for understanding market practice on base pay or pay structure.

- The deferred compensation data are not always reliable. For one thing, IRS rules require organizations to report deferred compensation the year it accrues and to report it again, despite the double counting, the year it is actually paid. Accordingly, deferred compensation that has accrued over several years is reported first at the time of accrual and then again when paid as a single very large lump sum. This is often seen in the year in which a chief executive retires. In addition, anecdotal evidence suggests that organizations do not uniformly report deferred compensation amounts.

- The data are at least a year old, and usually older. Organizations file at the end of the year, and organizations may also file extensions or delay in making the information publicly available. The 990 data are therefore likely to be a reasonable approximation of actual pay, but it is not the same as having contemporary information. The data must also be updated to present-day dollars before they can be used.

Despite these caveats, 990 data, properly understood and adjusted for inflation, are a relatively simple source of information on the pay practices of comparable organizations.

Publicly Available Surveys

Compensation survey information is made available to the public by both for-profit and nonprofit organizations. A representative list of organizations publishing national survey data is included in the resource list at the end of this book. WorldatWork (http://www.worldatwork.org), formerly the American Compensation Association, is an excellent source of information on survey sources.

National surveys include general compensation surveys, which typically have a nonprofit cut of the data, as well as surveys of the general nonprofit market and surveys of specific types of organizations in the nonprofit sector (for example, foundations, museums, international aid organizations). Local surveys will cover a single metropolitan area, a state, or a region; they may cover all organizations, all nonprofits, or a subset of nonprofits. In the Washington, DC area, for example, the National Capital Area Human Resources Association (HRA) publishes a detailed survey of Washington area compensation that includes a nonprofit cut. The Greater Washington Society of Association Executives (GWSAE) publishes an annual survey of association pay, and Cordom Associates publishes a general Washington, DC nonprofit survey.[11]

The data must usually be purchased from the organization publishing the survey — costs can range from as little as $50 to over $1,000 for the larger national surveys produced by the major compensation consulting firms. Special cuts of survey data are often available from the sponsoring organization, again for a fee. A special cut allows an organization to obtain data from the relevant subset of a larger group. Preferably, data from eight to 10 organizations should be included to make the results more meaningful.

Not all survey data are publicly available. Surveys are often conducted by a group of nonprofit organizations for their internal use, and the data are, in principle, available only to participants. However, nonparticipants can sometimes obtain the data by promising to participate in the next survey, or by requesting it from a friendly organization taking part in the survey.

Discovering what survey data are available can be challenging. Here are some suggestions for obtaining assistance:

- Contact groups and associations that might have conducted, or know of, compensation studies. These include local or regional associations of nonprofits, as well as associations of particular types of nonprofits. Some associations may be able to provide data on compensation at comparably sized for-profits as well.

- Do a Web search to find organizations that might collect compensation information for organizations of similar type or locality. Follow up with a phone call to help ensure that the organization is legitimate and that the data are up to date and reliable, and ask for references among other nonprofits.

- Ask similar organizations what survey data they know about or have. A group of similar organizations may be open to contracting for a targeted survey.

- Ask a compensation consultant for assistance. A good consultant will have access to the most important national surveys and will know how to find more specific surveys, such as by region or nonprofit type.

- Avoid data from headhunters and recruiters. Their data may not represent the overall market because they know the most about firms that are actively in the market; their data also may be skewed upward because they have an interest in getting as large a salary as possible for each of their recruits.

---

11. Human Resource Association of the National Capital Area. *2004 Compensation Survey Report – Vol. 1*; Greater Washington Society of Association Executives. *2004 GWSAE Association Compensation Survey Report*; Cordom Associates. *2004 Salary Survey of Nonprofit Organizations*.

- Avoid data available for free on the Web, unless the data come from a source that is known to be reputable. Free data are often self-reported without any check on accuracy and not always representative of the overall market.

Understanding and Using Survey Data

The survey data will be organized by position, and then by various cuts or subsets of the data. The chief executive position may be listed as "CEO," "Top Executive," "Executive Director," or some other (generally obvious) title. Please see the box on the following page for a breakdown of the data that may be included.

Using survey data is something of an art; this is one area where the assistance of an experienced professional can be especially helpful. The goal is to use the cut that is as close as possible to the market the organization has identified as its own. The problem is that the data are presented in discrete categories, but not necessarily with the desired crosscuts. For example, an organization might see its marketplace as a social welfare organization in the Southwest, of budget size $5 million to $10 million, with 50 employees, and a chief executive with 10 years' experience. The published data may include each of these cuts, but not a cut of all the factors taken together.

In some cases, the compensation committee may be able to purchase a special cut; if this is not possible, a simple approach is to take the single best cut. In the experience of the authors, budget size is the data cut most closely correlated, although by no means perfectly, with chief executive compensation. The next best cut is usually staff size. Adjustments for location or other factors may still be necessary if, for example, the organization is based in an area where compensation is significantly above or below the national average.

The compensation committee must also decide which quartile to use in determining the market. The most common approach is to target the median of the marketplace. In many cases the organization's compensation philosophy will provide considerable guidance by including a market target, again, probably most often the median of the marketplace. Targeting the median or lower is certainly the safest policy from a legal standpoint. An organization may choose to target above the median if the compensation committee can make a good case for the organization's need for special skills, experience, or leadership qualities. Such a case might exist in an organization that is repositioning itself, has ambitious growth plans, currently has an unusually skilled or experienced chief executive, or has a leading position within the community that justifies paying above the median of the market. However, targeting pay above the 75th percentile is unusual. Any organization targeting above the median should be able to explain its decision; a target above the 75th percentile should have an especially strong justification.

The organization's market target does not necessarily dictate, however, which data cut to use. While an organization targeting the median will generally use median data, using a higher or lower quartile can be another approach to adjusting the data. For example, if an organization is substantially larger than the highest budget cut in a survey, the 75th percentile may be closer to the organization's market than the survey median. In such a case, the compensation committee can use the 75th percentile as the unreported median of the organization's marketplace. This adjustment method should be used with caution, but it might also be appropriate with long-serving chief executives and in other cases where there are unusual factors that would differentiate the organization in question from the median organization in the survey.

SALARY SURVEY DATA

- **Base pay or base salary compensation:** The annual salary paid.

- **Extra cash compensation:** Any bonus or incentive paid.

- **Total cash compensation:** Salary plus any additional cash, generally bonus or incentive.

- **Fringe benefits:** Some surveys will report fringe benefits paid, often by type of benefit such as health insurance or free use of automobile. These are not always quantified, and the survey may simply report the existence or prevalence of the benefit.

- **Deferred compensation:** Compensation that is accrued but will be paid after the calendar year in which it is earned. Relatively rarely reported in standard surveys.

- **Total compensation:** If reported, this figure would include the cash value of all compensation, whether paid in the current year, deferred, or provided as a fringe benefit.

- **Location:** The number of organizations reporting from a particular location or region.

- **Organization type:** General compensation surveys will have a nonprofit category, which may or may not be further broken down. Nonprofit surveys may be broken down by type of nonprofit. These types include health and social welfare organizations, trade associations, advocacy organizations, professional associations, educational organizations, and others.

- **Organization budget:** This is generally grouped by category, for example, less than $5 million, $5 million to $10 million, and so on.

- **Time in position:** The number of years incumbents have been in the position.

- **Number of employees:** Usually grouped into categories.

- **The number of organizations reporting the particular data:** The number of organizations of a certain budget size, for example.

- **Quartiles:** Data are generally reported by quartile. Surveys commonly report three quartiles: the 25th percentile — the compensation amount above which 75 percent of all reported compensation data fall; the median or 50th percentile — the compensation amount above which 50 percent of all reported compensation data fall; and the third quartile or 75th percentile — the compensation amount above which 25 percent of all reported compensation data fall. Some surveys will also report the 10th percentile (90 percent of all data is higher), and the 90th percentile (10 percent of all data is higher).

- **The date of the information presented:** Surveys will show the effective date of the information they present.

Aging the Survey Data

All surveys will report when the data were collected; the data must then be updated to the present using an inflation factor. The compensation committee can do this using information from organizations that report annually on average increases in market pay. Good sources include the Conference Board (http://www.conference-board.org) and WorldatWork. Several of the larger compensation consulting firms, such as Mercer Human Resource Consulting and Hewitt Associates, also produce regular surveys of market pay movement (see Suggested Resources for more information).

SPECIAL SURVEYS

One of the best ways of gathering data — probably the very best if the right set of organizations can be found — is to conduct a special survey. With the right participants, a special survey will provide up-to-date data on organizations specifically chosen for their comparability. The IRS appears to favor this approach; its regulations specifically provide that smaller organizations (those with annual gross revenues of $1 million or less) may use compensation information from "three comparable organizations in the same or similar communities for similar services." Telephone calls are an acceptable way of gathering the information.[12]

However, some practical difficulties are involved in conducting a special survey:

- The organizations should be comparable in as many ways as possible, and identifying and securing the cooperation of a sufficient number of like organizations can be difficult.

- For the data to be statistically significant, the survey should include at least eight to 10 participants.

- In certain sectors (health care, for example) anti-trust issues may arise when organizations share compensation information. To minimize these, some authorities advise that the data be collected by an independent third party, that it be aggregated, and that at least five organizations participate in the survey.[13] Note, however, that where the data are publicly available on IRS Form 990s, the potential for antitrust issues may be lessened.

With these caveats in mind, however, organizing a special survey can benefit all the participants, especially if the survey is conducted on a regular basis.

Once the compensation committee has gathered sufficient data to meet the legal requirements and public expectations for understanding its target marketplace, it can move on to developing the elements of the organization's own compensation package. First, however, it should carefully review the legal standards for nonprofit chief executive compensation and ensure that the compensation level and structure it proposes will stand up to public scrutiny.

---

12. Internal Revenue Service. *Instructions for Form 990 and Form 990 E-Z 2003*. pp. 1, 12.

13. Department of Justice and Federal Trade Commission. *Statements of Antitrust Enforcement Policy in Health Care*. Washington, DC: Government Printing Office, 1996. John Davis (*Salary Surveys and Antitrust: An Overview for the HR Professional*, Scottsdale, AZ: WorldatWork, 2003) notes that this guideline is generally accepted in industries other than health care.

6.
Meeting the Legal Standards

One of the board's most important responsibilities when setting chief executive pay is to ensure that the compensation level and structure meet the legal standards set by the IRS for tax-exempt organizations. If an organization does not adhere to these standards, the organization, its board members, and its senior staff may be penalized. The board must also ensure that the organization meets the IRS reporting requirements and any applicable laws of the state in which it is organized.

To ensure compliance, compensation committee members need first to understand the IRS's purpose in setting the standards and the definitions it uses in doing so. The IRS's purpose is to ensure that nonprofit organizations operate in ways that qualify them for tax exemption and to provide a legal guideline for making that determination. The standards apply to the types of organizations described in sections 501(a) and 501(c)(1)-(27) of the Internal Revenue Code (IRC), which the IRS terms *tax-exempt* or *exempt* organizations.

PRIVATE INUREMENT

Private inurement is the diversion of an organization's assets or income to persons, generally insiders, who have not earned or merited it.[14] Federal tax law differentiates nonprofit organizations from for-profit organizations by forbidding nonprofits from engaging in private inurement. Insiders engage in private inurement when they turn a nonprofit into a profit-making enterprise for themselves. In the IRS's own words:

> [P]rivate inurement is likely to arise where the financial benefit represents a transfer of the organization's financial resources to an individual solely by virtue of the individual's relationship with the organization, and without regard to accomplishing exempt purposes.[15]

The IRS's private inurement doctrine forbids all tax-exempt organizations from providing income or assets to persons with a significant relationship with the organization (insiders) for their own private purposes. Private foundations, which are not subject to the intermediate sanctions regulations described below, are subject to restrictions on excessive compensation under the private inurement doctrine and also under the IRS's rules against *self-dealing*: transactions where someone who is in a fiduciary relationship with an organization acquires or makes use of property that belongs to the organization for his or her own benefit. The self-dealing rules completely forbid certain transactions — leasing of property, for example — between insiders and a private foundation, but do allow compensation of insiders, so long as it is not excessive.

---

14. This discussion of private inurement and intermediate sanctions is based on Bruce Hopkins, *The Law of Intermediate Sanctions* (New York: John Wiley & Sons, 2003), and on an unpublished paper by Celia Roady of Morgan, Lewis & Bockius, on intermediate sanctions for the ALI-ABA Course of Study, Tax-Exempt Charitable Organizations, November 22, 2002.

15. IRS General Counsel Memorandum 38459, cited in Bruce Hopkins, *The Law of Intermediate Sanctions* (New York: John Wiley & Sons, 2003), p. 24.

The private inurement doctrine has two main implications for chief executive compensation at all tax-exempt organizations:

1. Compensation should be clearly tied to the chief executive's performance in leading the organization toward achievement of its mission ("accomplishing exempt purposes").

2. Because there is no equity available in a nonprofit organization, compensation committees should be wary of any compensation arrangement feature that looks like the distribution of profits.

INTERMEDIATE SANCTIONS

The law introducing intermediate sanctions (IRC Section 4958) was enacted by Congress in 1996 in response to perceived abuses of nonprofit status. The sanctions are *intermediate* because they fall between revocation of tax-exempt status, the drastic but only penalty for abuse of the status before 1996, and no penalty at all. By providing for usable penalties, Congress hoped to strengthen IRS oversight of nonprofit organizations and their dealings with insiders.

The IRS intermediate sanctions regulations apply to a subset of all nonprofits: IRC 501(c)(3) public charities and 501(c)(4) social welfare organizations. The IRS refers to these organizations as *applicable tax-exempt organizations*. The regulations penalize a disqualified person if he or she receives excess compensation from an applicable organization. A *disqualified person* is someone who is in a position to exercise substantial influence with respect to the organization's affairs. Disqualified persons include presidents, chief executives, chief operating officers, treasurers, chief financial officers, other key employees, board members, close relatives of officers and board members, and others (such as founders) who are in a position to influence the organization.

Neither the private inurement doctrine nor the intermediate sanctions regulations forbids financial relationships between nonprofit organizations and insiders. Instead, both require that the organization receive in return a benefit more or less equal to the financial gain to the insider. The intermediate sanctions regulations are to a large extent a codification of this doctrine: In transactions between an insider/disqualified person and a nonprofit, there must be a substantially equal exchange of benefits.

To be subject to intermediate sanctions, a transaction must meet a three-part test:

1. The organization involved must be an applicable tax-exempt organization: a 501(c)(3) public charity or a 501(c)(4) social welfare organization.

2. The transaction must involve a disqualified person.

3. An *excess benefit transaction* must have taken place. An excess benefit transaction is a form of private inurement; it is a "transaction in which an economic benefit is provided by an applicable tax-exempt organization, directly or indirectly, to or for the use of a disqualified person, and the value of the economic benefit provided by the organization exceeds *the value of the consideration (including the performance of services) received for providing the benefit*" [emphasis added].[16] In other words, it is a transaction in which the insider gets more from the nonprofit organization than the nonprofit receives in return.

---

16. Internal Revenue Service. *Instructions for Form 990 and Form 990 E-Z 2003.* p. 11; Bruce Hopkins. *The Law of Intermediate Sanctions.* New York: John Wiley & Sons, 2003.

If a transaction is judged subject to intermediate sanctions, the IRS may impose penalties on both the individual disqualified person involved and on organization officials[17]:

- The disqualified person owes a penalty of 25 percent of the excess benefit, that is, the amount found to be in excess of a reasonable benefit in exchange for the services provided. The person must correct (i.e., repay) the excess benefit within 90 days after the date of mailing of a notice of deficiency.[18] Failure to correct the excess benefit makes the disqualified person subject to a 200 percent penalty.

- Organization officials, including board members, chief executives, and officers, who "knowingly, willfully, and without reasonable cause" participate in an excess benefit transaction are subject to a 10 percent penalty with a total cap of $10,000 for all persons involved. The penalty is not imposed on the organization, but on the individuals themselves. In other words, board members are personally liable.

As a compensation committee develops its chief executive compensation package, it must pay close attention to the definitions and interpretations used by the IRS. The IRS defines compensation to include all economic benefits other than certain nontaxable fringe benefits and other small, technical categories, and uses a *reasonableness* standard in determining whether a particular compensation arrangement is an excess benefit. Reasonableness is defined as "the value that would ordinarily be paid for like services by like enterprises under like circumstances."[19] The legislative history of IRC Section 4958 and other commentary give some additional guidance on what is meant by reasonableness and therefore on what should be included in a compensation analysis to pass IRS muster. The criteria include

1. Compensation paid by similarly situated organizations, taxable and nontaxable, for functionally comparable positions. There is a preference for organizations in the same community or region.

2. The need of the organization for the service of the individual being compensated.

3. The relation of the individual's compensation to that of other employees in the organization.

4. The individual's duties and performance history.

5. The individual's prior compensation history.

6. The location of the organization.

7. Written offers from similar institutions for the services of the individual involved.

8. Whether there was arm's length bargaining, that is, approval by an independent board or committee of the board.

9. The individual's background, education, training, experience, and responsibilities.

10. The size and complexity of the organization in terms of assets, income, and number of employees.

11. The amount of time the individual devotes to the position.[20]

---

17. Internal Revenue Service. *Instructions for Form 990 and Form 990 E-Z 2003*. p. 13.

18. IRC § 6212.

19. Internal Revenue Service. *Instructions for Form 990 and Form 990 E-Z 2003*. p. 12.

20. Bruce Hopkins. *The Law of Intermediate Sanctions*. New York: John Wiley & Sons, 2003.

Any analysis presented to the board should cover as many of the factors listed on the previous page as are applicable, and explain those factors in clearly understandable terms. None of the factors is dispositive by itself. In the experience of the authors, the most important factors to consider as part of a market analysis are the pay practices of similar organizations; the size and complexity of the organization; the pay practices in the organization's region or locality; and the duties of the employee. However, to date there is not enough experience with the IRS's application of the standards to understand which factors they consider in practice to be most important.

REVENUE SHARING, INCENTIVES, AND BONUSES

Compensation arrangements that are at least in part based on the revenues of the organization are permissible under intermediate sanctions, as are incentives and bonuses, so long as their total amount is reasonable. The IRS accepts that gain-sharing and other incentive plans can benefit a nonprofit organization, but the organization must receive proportionate benefit from gain-sharing or incentive plans. Compensation committees should be especially careful in scrutinizing such arrangements and considering the maximum amount that might be earned. The committee may want to include a cap on compensation under such arrangements in order to ensure compliance with the law. The cap should be set using market comparison to identify a reasonable total cash compensation level. In addition, compensation committees should be aware of the ethical issues associated with paying the chief executive a percentage of the organization's total revenue. These issues are discussed further in Chapter 8.

INITIAL CONTRACT EXCEPTION

An arm's-length contract negotiated for a new hire is exempt from intermediate sanctions, under the theory that the new hire is not a disqualified person because he or she does not yet have influence with the organization — arm's length negotiation is critical. This general principle has three modifiers:

1. Any contingent arrangement such as a bonus must be outside the control of the disqualified person; thus a bonus based on board discretion is not exempt from intermediate sanctions and will be judged by the usual reasonableness standard. A bonus that is based entirely on factors beyond the person's control, such as hitting certain preset revenue targets, is exempt, however.

2. There must be substantial performance from the person involved.[21]

3. There must be a written contract between the organization and the new chief executive that is executed *before* he or she is hired.

THE REBUTTABLE PRESUMPTION OF REASONABLENESS

Congress, wanting to encourage boards to follow sound procedures in setting compensation, established guidelines on those procedures; if those guidelines are followed, there is a presumption that a compensation arrangement is reasonable. This *rebuttable presumption of reasonableness* shifts the burden of proof to the IRS in

---

21. Internal Revenue Service. *Instructions for Form 990 and Form 990 E-Z 2003*. p. 12.

showing that an excess benefit transaction has taken place (that is, in rebutting the presumption). In order to fall under the rebuttable presumption of reasonableness, a compensation arrangement must meet three conditions[22]:

1. It must be approved in advance by an authorized body of the tax-exempt organization, composed entirely of individuals with no conflict of interest with respect to the compensation arrangement. This can include the governing body of the organization (i.e., its board), a committee of the governing body as allowed by state law, or other parties as allowed by state law.

2. The authorized body must obtain and rely on appropriate data as to comparability prior to making a determination. Data are appropriate if, "given the knowledge and expertise of the board's members, it has information sufficient to determine whether, under the valuation standards, the compensation arrangement in its entirety is reasonable or the property transfer at fair market value."[23] Appropriate sources and types of data are described in Chapter 5; the data must be presented in a way that allows a reasoned judgment on the part of the board, by showing how the criteria for reasonableness, such as compensation at organizations that are comparable in terms of mission, location, size, and complexity, have been applied. For organizations with $1 million or less in gross annual revenue, however, "appropriate comparability data includes data on compensation paid by three comparable organizations in the same or similar communities for similar services."[24]

3. The authorized body must adequately document the basis for its determination at the same time that the determination is made. This documentation must include

   a. the terms of the transaction

   b. the date

   c. the members of the body present during debate and those voting

   d. the comparability data obtained and relied on by the authorized body and how the data was obtained

   e. any actions by a member of the body with a conflict of interest

   f. documentation must take place within 60 days of the final actions or the next meeting of the body, whichever is later

   g. after documentation within 60 days, it must be approved by the authorized body within a "reasonable" time

The IRS urges nonprofits to comply as much as possible with the rebuttable presumption of reasonableness standards, even if they cannot fully meet the requirements,[25] implying that even partial compliance will help in establishing the reasonableness of a compensation arrangement. Satisfaction of the rebuttal presumption of reasonableness will also protect managers from personal liability.

22. Bruce Hopkins. *The Law of Intermediate Sanctions*. New York: John Wiley & Sons, 2003; Internal Revenue Service. *Instructions for Form 990 and Form 990 E-Z 2003*. p. 12.

23. Bruce Hopkins. *The Law of Intermediate Sanctions*. New York: John Wiley & Sons, 2003. p. 165.

24. Internal Revenue Service. *Instructions for Form 990 and Form 990 E-Z 2003*. p. 12.

25. Internal Revenue Service. *Instructions for Form 990 and Form 990 E-Z 2003*. p. 13.

A Second Protection from Personal Liability

Beyond the rebuttable presumption of reasonableness, managers of nonprofit organizations, including board members, have a second protection from personal liability under intermediate sanctions. Personal liability requires *knowing* participation in an excess benefit transaction; managers are held not to be knowing participants if they relied on a reasoned written opinion from a professional with respect to the elements of a transaction within the professional's expertise. The opinion must recite both the facts and the applicable standards. Professionals can include legal counsel with respect to the legal standards to be followed, but on compensation issues per se professionals are

> independent valuation experts who (1) hold themselves out to the public as appraisers or compensation consultants, (2) perform the relevant valuations on a regular basis, (3) are qualified to make valuations of the type of property or services involved, and (4) include in the written opinion a certification that the foregoing three requirements are met.[26]

The intermediate sanctions regulations set up a clear three-step process for boards to follow to ensure compliance with the law:

1. Set up a formal process for setting compensation.

2. Obtain carefully researched comparable data on chief executive pay.

3. Document the decision-making process thoroughly.

The regulations seem complicated, but they should not be excessively burdensome if organizations are careful about following these three steps. Fundamentally, the intermediate sanctions regulations put into law a principle that any responsible board should already be following: paying the chief executive as much as necessary for the services provided, but no more than is justified by the market. The law sets out what is in fact a common-sense standard for defining the marketplace — a standard more or less identical to the one the authors would recommend be used even in the absence of intermediate sanctions. In fact, those nonprofits that are not explicitly subject to intermediate sanctions face similar legal requirements and are well advised to act in accordance with the intermediate sanctions standards.

IRS Form 990 Reporting

The IRS requires almost all nonprofit organizations to file annual IRS Form 990 tax returns (the most prominent exceptions are certain religious and governmental organizations). For officers, including the chief executive, organizations are required to report the following[27]:

❏ Salaries, fees, bonuses, and severance payments. Current year payment of amounts reported as deferred compensation in previous years must also be reported in the year received. In other words, deferred compensation will appear *twice* in an organization's 990 reports — in the year when it is earned, and in the year when it is received. This is troubling to some organizations, since it can give the uninformed reader a false impression about the total amount of

---

26. Bruce Hopkins. *The Law of Intermediate Sanctions*. New York: John Wiley & Sons, 2003. p. 188.

27. Internal Revenue Service. *Instructions for Form 990 and Form 990 E-Z 2003*. pp. 27-28.

compensation. Organizations can, and should, attach an explanation of such payments to their 990 forms.

❑ All forms of deferred compensation and future severance payments, whether or not funded or vested, as well as payments to welfare benefit plans, such as medical, life insurance, and disability.

❑ Taxable and nontaxable fringe benefits, such as the value of automobiles and housing provided, as well as expense accounts and expense reimbursements.

The requirement to report fringe benefits can be a trap for the unwary nonprofit because the IRS will treat unreported compensation as an "automatic" excess benefit transaction, even if it would otherwise be reasonable under the intermediate sanctions regulations. Thus, if an organization were to pay for spouse travel on a business trip, intending it as part of the compensation to the chief executive, but did not report the benefit on the organization's 990 or the individual's W-2 or Form 1099, and the individual did not report it on the individual income tax filing, the payment would automatically be considered an excess benefit transaction.[28]

An organization that is subject to the intermediate sanctions regulations is also required to report "any Section 4958 excess benefit transactions"[29] during the tax year, and any from past years of which it became aware. The implication of this is that even though the intermediate sanctions penalties are paid by individuals, the organization can be harmed because it must publicly report and acknowledge involvement in a prohibited transaction.

COMPLYING WITH STATE LAW

Because they are formed as nonprofit corporations under state law, nonprofits are subject to state, as well as federal, regulation and reporting requirements, and they have come under increasing scrutiny by state attorneys general in recent years. As a general rule, states follow the IRS regulations with respect to chief executive compensation, and a board that ensures compliance with federal regulations will meet state standards as well.

THE IMPORTANCE OF LEGAL COUNSEL

Given the increased level of scrutiny by both state and federal authorities and the increasing complexity of many nonprofit compensation plans, the authors recommend that organizations seek advice from experienced independent counsel when structuring both their decision-making process and their compensation plan. Legal advice is especially important if compensation is complex or if it appears to be high by community standards or in comparison to past pay practices at the organization.

---

28. Lawrence M. Brauer and Leonard J. Henzke, Jr. "Automatic Excess Benefit Transactions Under IRC 4958." http://www.irs.gov/pub/irs-tege/eotopice04.pdf.

29. Internal Revenue Service. *Instructions for Form 990 and Form 990 E-Z 2003.* p. 32.

7.
Passing the Test of Public and Stakeholder Scrutiny

As strict as federal and state legal standards may be, an even more rigorous standard for judging chief executive pay is the test of public and stakeholder opinion. As Fisher Howe observes,

> The accountability of nonprofit organizations is principally to the public — a formless entity to which boards somehow owe a fiduciary answerability. In large measure, therefore, unless things go awry, boards and board members answer to their own consciences before the public and to their own self-determined principles of what is right and good.[30]

Boards must be fully prepared to explain and justify their organizations' chief executive compensation packages to the media, the general public, and the organization's stakeholders. Not only is this information available in the public domain, it is the subject of public interest. The press is increasing the level of its investigative reporting on nonprofits, and reporters and others have access to the chief executive pay figures reported on each organization's IRS Form 990. These forms are increasingly available on the Web; many organizations post their own, and virtually all can be obtained through Guidestar (www.guidestar.org).

Perceptions of pay practices are, of course, strongly influenced by the chief executive's experience, credentials, and performance; a long-serving chief executive who is universally recognized for strong performance faces different public expectations than an obscure and untested new hire. No matter what the chief executive's background, however, the compensation package needs to pass the front page test: How comfortable will board members be if every detail of the chief executive's pay package is published on the front page of the local newspaper? In the case of larger nonprofits, how comfortable will board members be if the front page in question is that of the *New York Times*, the *Wall Street Journal*, the *Los Angeles Times*, or the *Washington Post*?

In setting chief executive compensation, the compensation committee must be especially sensitive to the perceptions and expectations of those most likely to take an interest in the organization's pay practices, including donors, volunteers and other supporters, and the organization's staff. Donors seek assurance that their money is being used wisely and effectively, and volunteers seek assurance that they are giving their time to a worthy organization. Members of both groups may perceive apparently high pay levels as diversions of funds that could or should be going to the organization's mission. These stakeholders may also have expectations based on the mission and history of the organization; some types of nonprofits, such as advocacy organizations, groups working with the poor or underprivileged, and groups with a religious affiliation or origin, may be expected by supporters, staff, and the public to pay more modestly.

---

30. Fisher Howe. *The Nonprofit Leadership Team*. San Francisco: Jossey-Bass, 2004. p. 154.

Stakeholders are particularly sensitive to mixed signals transmitted by the compensation committee or the board, especially when the board's words send one message and its actions send another. An example comes from the United Way of the National Capital Area, which hired Charles Anderson as its executive director in early 2003. Anderson succeeded interim director Robert Egger, who had taken a much-below-market $85,000 a year salary during his tenure. In August 2004, according to the *Washington Post*, "the board of directors quietly voted [Anderson] a $25,000 raise, on top of his $190,000 annual salary ... Even those who approved of the raise said the decision should have been announced. 'We were going to be a transparent organization,' said Harriet Guttenberg, former chairman of the Montgomery United Way advisory council." In fact, the board had justification for the raise: "Board member John T. Schwieters said Anderson was underpaid compared with chief executives of other United Ways and local nonprofits of similar size. 'I thought it was important to recognize the stress and strain he's been under ... and bring him up to the level of other people,' Schwieters said."[31] However, many of the organization's stakeholders felt that this reasoning had not been conveyed before the raise was announced. If the board had acted in accordance with its stated goal of transparency, it might have averted much of the negative feeling that the raise engendered among its key stakeholders.

INTERNAL STAKEHOLDERS: THE STAFF

Organization staff members form a pivotal stakeholder group, and the compensation committee must consider the organization's current compensation structure for all of its employees when developing the chief executive's compensation package. Compensation sends a powerful message to staff about the board's priorities for the organization and its regard for the employees who carry out the organization's mission. When the compensation committee sets chief executive compensation without regard to the pay levels of other employees or without giving employees a rationale for its decisions, it tells employees that it does not consider them important stakeholders. When the compensation committee allows a major disparity between chief executive compensation and the compensation structure for other staff, it tells employees that it thinks the chief executive is crucial to realization of the organization's mission, and staff members are relatively unimportant. By contrast, when the compensation committee can demonstrate that the chief executive compensation package is part of a coherent overall pay system, it tells employees that the entire staff is part of a team and that the committee takes seriously its accountability to all of the organization's stakeholders.

Staff members expect that the chief executive's pay will be broadly consistent with the pay levels and compensation structure for the rest of the organization and with the chief executive compensation offered in the past. Broadly consistent does not mean identical; it means logical given the existing compensation structure and the culture of the organization. The chief executive's pay will in almost all cases be higher than that of other employees, but it should not be disproportionately higher. (Common exceptions: Athletic coaches and professors of medicine are paid more than the president at some universities. Persons in revenue-generating positions at

31. Jacqueline L. Salmon. "United Way Chief Toils to Resuscitate Charity." *Washington Post*, November 1, 2004.

some nonprofits can also earn more than the chief executive, at least in good years.) In the authors' experience, the chief executive salary is set at most 60 to 70 percent above that of the next highest paid employee. Boards also need to bear in mind that chief executives can be paid too little in comparison to their staff. Chief executive pay that is much below market may compress pay for senior staff. This can result in poor morale and the loss of key employees.

The chief executive compensation package may also include elements that are not made available to other employees, such as a bonus or incentive; or bonus or incentive pay may be set at higher levels for the chief executive than for other staff. Chief executives and other highly compensated employees may have certain perquisites or benefits not available to other staff, including deferred compensation or special retirement arrangements. Again, however, these should not be so large as to be inconsistent with the organization's culture and practices or with the expectations of the local community. Of course, the total package must be consistent with the marketplace to meet legal standards.

WHAT IS THE PUBLIC PERCEPTION?

Meeting the test of public scrutiny means being accountable to donors, staff, and the public. However, when developing its chief executive compensation package, the compensation committee needs to go beyond acting out of self-preservation. The committee's goal should be not merely to develop a package that it can defend against legal scrutiny and public questioning, but to take advantage of the opportunity to make a positive statement about the organization.

This is where the work that the compensation committee has done in reviewing the organization's mission, priorities, and objectives becomes an asset. A compensation committee that can set its organization's chief executive compensation package in the context of the organization's vision for the future and the outcomes that it hopes to achieve is in a good position to make a positive public impression, and it need not be hesitant to announce the compensation terms once the new chief executive is hired.

The best way of judging potential public reaction to chief executive compensation is for compensation committee members to use their own experience with the organization and the community to predict how the package they are planning will be perceived.

The last test is perhaps the best one: The board should have no reticence about making its compensation decision fully public before it appears on the 990 form. A commitment to this level of candor helps an organization maintain its integrity, because it ensures that the board will ask itself about public reaction to its compensation practices. Taking the test of public scrutiny seriously has another advantage as well: A compensation package that is acceptable to the public is almost certain to pass legal muster also.

WHAT SHOULD COMMITTEE MEMBERS CONSIDER WHEN PLANNING A COMPENSATION PACKAGE?

Committee members should ask themselves the following questions:

- What would my reaction as a member of the community be if a comparable local nonprofit compensated its chief executive at the proposed level?

- What is the history and nature of this nonprofit, and what constraints might that put on pay?

- What expectations do staff members have about the chief executive's pay level? How will the staff react to this pay package? How does the pay of high achieving staff members compare with the proposed chief executive pay? How would I react if I were one of those staff people?

- Is there any reason to think that the organization may be under press scrutiny for any of its practices aside from chief executive pay?

- How is the chief executive perceived, or likely to be perceived? If the chief executive's compensation were questioned, what credentials or performance record would I as a board member point to in order to justify the proposed compensation?

- How can I as a board member explain the chief executive's compensation in relation to the organization's mission, priorities, and objectives?

- How comfortable would I as a board member be in publicizing the proposed compensation arrangement? How comfortable do I think the chief executive would be?

8.
Understanding the Elements of Compensation

We now come to the heart of the matter: establishing the appropriate salary level and compensation plan for the chief executive. By the time the compensation committee has reached this stage, it will have worked through the series of steps outlined in the preceding chapters in order to ensure that its compensation decisions meet the tests of legal and public scrutiny:

- Establishing a process for setting executive compensation

- Reviewing the organization's mission, priorities, and objectives and the chief executive's role in achieving them

- Establishing a compensation philosophy

- Developing a title, job description, and profile for the chief executive

- Reviewing the organization's marketplace and learning what level of compensation is consistent with it

- Understanding the legal constraints on chief executive compensation and on the board process for setting it, especially the IRS private inurement and intermediate sanctions regulations

- Understanding the constraints that the nature and history of the organization, and any public or other stakeholder concerns, might place on chief executive compensation, and the opportunity that chief executive compensation presents for sending a message about the organization's mission and priorities

The compensation committee must now decide how it wants to structure the chief executive compensation package. The elements of a compensation package are base salary; extra cash compensation, such as bonus or incentive awards; retirement and savings plans; deferred compensation; sign-on and retention bonuses; and other benefits and perquisites. The compensation committee must identify the elements that it wishes to incorporate and those that it cannot or will not include. It must also identify the parameters beyond which it cannot or will not go in terms of salary level, perquisites, and other elements of the compensation package before it enters negotiations with individual chief executive candidates. Finally, the board should consider how it will assess annual performance and award bonuses and incentives, if those are part of the compensation package. It also must determine how it will make annual adjustments in salary, and the data and procedures it will use in making those adjustments.

BASE SALARY AND ANNUAL SALARY ADJUSTMENTS

Base salary is defined as annual compensation exclusive of all one-time or contingent payments. Base salary is the one element common to all compensation packages, and makes up the lion's share of total compensation in almost all nonprofit compensation packages. In fact, for the majority of nonprofits, base salary is likely to be the only compensation element other than benefits. It is thus especially important that base salary be set appropriately.

Research on the organization's marketplace will have given the compensation committee an idea of the typical base salary for chief executives at comparable organizations; review of the organization's culture, its compensation history for chief executives and other staff, and its current financial picture will have helped the committee determine whether matching market norms is feasible and desirable. This information taken together enables the compensation committee to set a target base salary amount and a range within which it is willing and able to negotiate with a chief executive candidate.

The base salary amount will also depend on whether or not the organization chooses to include a bonus or incentive element. In looking at the marketplace, the organization should compare the proposed total cash compensation for the chief executive (base salary plus bonus or incentive) to market total cash for its marketplace. An organization may choose to offer a higher base salary and no bonus or incentive, or a lower base salary with a bonus or incentive; but in either case the total package should be benchmarked against market total cash for the organization's marketplace.

One common way to set the base salary is to place it within a market-based salary range. While the size of salary ranges differs from organization to organization, in the most common model the salary range extends from 80 percent to 120 percent of the market point for the position. Thus, if the organization has determined from its research that the median of the marketplace is $100,000, the salary range based on this median would go from $80,000 to $120,000.

Initial salary is not necessarily at the center or target of a salary range. In fact, standard compensation practice is to bring in new employees somewhat below the center of the range, so that they move up through the range as they receive annual merit pay increases. However, a compensation committee can also use the salary range to recognize the experience and past performance levels of stronger chief executive candidates by dividing the range into three segments.

Minimum	Target Range		Maximum
20% Below Target	5% Below Market	5% Above Market	20% Above Target
Developmental	Full Performance and Experience		Outstanding

Most chief executive candidates will likely have skills and competencies that are fully developed and will have performed consistently in positions of responsibility in the past. For such candidates, base pay can be set within the target range, from 5 percent below to 5 percent above market. For a chief executive candidate whose skills and competencies are still developing, the compensation committee might offer a base salary that is as much as 20 percent below the target. For a chief executive candidate whose background and experience are exceptional, the compensation committee might offer a base salary that is above the target, although this allows less room for future salary growth. This procedure gives compensation committees a way to quantify the concept of "salary commensurate with experience" without straying too far from market norms.

In addition to setting base pay, the compensation committee must determine how annual salary adjustments will be made. Nonprofit organizations typically adjust the chief executive's salary annually to reflect both performance and movement in the marketplace. Market movement for salaries is similar, but not identical to, general inflation; even in a low or no inflation economy, salaries will generally move upward. It is thus important to obtain data specifically on salary trends in the organization's marketplace, and not to depend on inflation data such as the Consumer Price Index, to determine an appropriate salary adjustment. Organizations compiling such data include WorldatWork, the Conference Board, and several of the large human resources consulting firms (see Suggested Resources on page 77 for a comprehensive list).

Annual salary adjustments may also be tied to the chief executive's performance. The central function of the performance review is to help the chief executive build on recognized strengths and improve performance in identified areas of need — based on previously determined performance goals that are both *institutional* and *individually* tied to the chief executive who is being assessed and may be held personally accountable. However, in the current environment of scrutiny of executive pay practices, the performance review also serves another key function. Tying executive salary adjustments and bonuses to the performance review has the desirable outcome of demonstrating a solid rationale for executive compensation decisions.

The best way to link compensation to performance is to decide *before* the evaluation takes place what rewards will be associated with achieving the organization's objectives and communicate that decision to the chief executive. For example, the board could agree with the chief executive that achieving stated objectives would mean (finances allowing) a certain percentage increase in salary, or the award of an incentive amount. Going beyond the objectives would be worth more.

In the absence of an existing link between pay and performance, the next best thing is to decide on an appropriate reward (a salary increase, an ad hoc bonus, or some combination of the two) and carefully explain to the chief executive the particular achievements that justify the increase or bonus. That explanation could then serve as the basis for the following year's performance plan.

For compensation committees that elect to tie annual compensation adjustments to performance, the salary range provides a way to determine appropriate increments. In such cases, individual increases depend on two factors: position in range and performance. All other things being equal, persons low in the range receive larger increases because they are further below the market, and persons with stronger performance receive larger increases than weaker performers. Thus a person whose salary was below the midpoint in year 1, and whose performance was excellent, would receive an increase (including cost of living adjustment) that moved base salary closer to the year 2 midpoint. On the other hand, a person whose salary was above the midpoint in year 1, and whose performance was excellent, would receive an increase, but the overall percentage (including cost of living adjustment) would be lower than the percentage for the person whose salary was below the midpoint, so that year 2 salary would remain within the appropriate salary range.

In developing the chief executive compensation package, the compensation committee must be able to state clearly what the base salary range will be and how annual salary adjustments will be calculated. If salary increases are to be tied to performance, the committee must also be able to articulate how often evaluation will occur and what the evaluation process will entail. (For more information on the evaluation process, please see *Assessment of the Chief Executive* on page 81.)

BONUSES, INCENTIVES, AND OTHER ANNUAL CASH COMPENSATION AWARDS

After base salary, the next most common element in chief executive compensation is some type of extra cash compensation in the form of an annual bonus or incentive. There is no bright line distinction between the terms *bonus* and *incentive*, but a bonus often refers to an amount awarded at the discretion of the board based on its subjective judgment of performance, while an incentive is an annual cash amount that can be earned by meeting agreed-upon performance targets.

The inclusion of extra cash compensation for chief executives is becoming increasingly common among nonprofit organizations. It is more common among larger organizations, and is seen most often in health care-related organizations, associations, nonprofit media organizations, and other nonprofits that compete for talent with the for-profit sector. Extra cash compensation for chief executives is less common among foundations and advocacy organizations.

Estimates of the percentage of nonprofits with chief executive bonus or incentive programs vary depending on the survey. A 2003 Quatt Associates survey of major nonprofits showed that 46.2 percent offered such programs; the Buck Consultants *2002 Not-For-Profit Compensation and Benefits Survey* found that 39.1 percent of organizations offered such programs; the Mercer *2004 Executive Compensation Survey* showed that 24.1 percent offered bonus or incentive programs.[32]

If offered, bonuses and incentives are generally paid annually, but incentives can also be structured over a longer term, with payment delayed for more than a year. This kind of incentive is a form of *deferred compensation*. Long-term incentives are used to encourage retention (the incentive is paid after a specified number of years to encourage the chief executive to stay with the organization), for the achievement of multiyear objectives (e.g., the achievement of an ambitious budget growth objective), or both.

A compensation committee may choose to pay part of a chief executive's total compensation in the form of a bonus or incentive for several reasons:

- **Recognition of achievement:** Boards often like to have the ability to recognize extraordinary achievement by providing a bonus. The bonus might be awarded at the end of a successful year, or upon achieving an important organizational objective. Boards need to be careful in how they award ad hoc bonuses, however. The amount paid must be in line with organizational and community expectations and legal standards. Even an ad hoc bonus should still be tied to identifiable achievements; otherwise, there is a risk that the bonus will simply become an entitlement. A bonus that is not tied to particular achievements is also less motivating, since it is not clear what behavior or successes are being rewarded.

- **Performance focus and motivation:** Extra cash compensation plans can be used to identify key objectives and encourage chief executive and organizational performance. In such plans, the accomplishment of key objectives is rewarded with incentive pay.

- **Market competitiveness:** Especially with larger nonprofits, or with chief executives coming from the for-profit sector, market-based expectations for a bonus opportunity may exist.

---

32. Buck Consultants. *2002 Not-For-Profit Compensation and Benefits Survey*. p. 66; Mercer. *2004 Executive Compensation Survey*. p. 100.000.112; Quatt Associates. *2004 Not-for-Profit Compensation Survey*. p. 8.

- **Management of compensation costs:** An incentive or bonus is a way to align total chief executive compensation with the market without committing the organization to paying the full amount in fixed base salary. In a bad year the organization can cut or forgo the bonus without having to reduce base salary. Annual salary increases can also be more moderate, reducing fixed costs over the long run.

Bonus and incentive amounts at nonprofits are relatively modest by the standards of for-profit organizations. Recent surveys have found a median chief executive bonus amount of 15 to 22 percent of base salary for those organizations that provide extra cash compensation.[33] In the authors' experience, incentive percentages can be as low as 5 percent of base salary; they are rarely higher than 25 to 30 percent of base. The board should explicitly budget for extra cash compensation if it has a reasonable expectation that the extra cash will be awarded.

Bonus and incentive plans can be structured with varying degrees of formality. Tying the incentive plan to the achievement of organizational objectives can effectively encourage organizational and chief executive performance by ensuring a focus on the organization's key goals. The financial reward is less important than the fact that the incentive plan motivates and focuses the chief executive.

As the basis for determining incentive eligibility, the board and the chief executive should set annual performance goals. Using the balanced scorecard approach described in Chapter 2, the chief executive and the board can establish goals in five key areas: mission, internal excellence and operations, constituent or stakeholder satisfaction, innovation and learning for future excellence and viability, and financial status.[34] The board and the chief executive then formally review performance in relation to these goals at the end of each year, and the board uses the results of the review to determine both incentive eligibility and eligibility for a base pay increase beyond the cost of living adjustment. The board may weight all the goals equally or weight some more heavily than others, depending on its priorities for the year.

In setting financial objectives, the board should be careful about directly awarding a percentage of money raised. Incentives structured in this way are considered unethical by many nonprofits and may attract extra scrutiny from the IRS. The Association of Fundraising Professionals prohibits its members from receiving such compensation and states that, where compensation is percentage based, "charitable mission can become secondary to self-gain" and "there is incentive for self-dealing to prevail over donors' best interests."[35] As noted previously, setting a cap on revenue-based incentives can help ensure that the total paid does not create intermediate sanctions concerns.

When properly structured and handled, an incentive plan can be a very useful management tool for a nonprofit. However, not all incentive plans work. Without careful and continuing board involvement, an incentive plan can simply become an

33. Buck Consultants. *2002 Not-For-Profit Compensation and Benefits Survey*. p. 66; Quatt Associates. *2004 Not-for-Profit Compensation Survey*. p. 8.

34. Robert S. Kaplan and David P. Norton. *Translating Strategy into Action: The Balanced Scorecard*. Boston: Harvard Business School Press, 1996.

35. Association of Fundraising Professionals. "Position Paper: Percentage-Based Compensation." (Retrieved February 11, 2005, from http://www.afpnet.org/tier3_cd.cfm?folder_id=899&content_item_id=1227).

automatic addition to base salary. Once an incentive becomes an entitlement, it loses its ability to motivate the chief executive. In addition, a carelessly managed incentive plan can destroy morale among other nonprofit staff: If the chief executive receives an annual bonus whether or not the organization can point to identifiable achievements, staff may see the bonus as simply an extra, and undeserved, senior management perk. If a bonus or incentive plan is to be motivational and strategic, the board must be involved in setting objectives and must be rigorous in judging organizational and chief executive performance.

DETERMINING IF EXTRA CASH COMPENSATION MAKES SENSE FOR THE ORGANIZATION

The following questions should be asked by the compensation committee before taking the next step in creating an incentive program:

- Does the chief executive expect extra cash compensation as part of a competitive compensation package?

- Is providing extra cash compensation customary in the nonprofit's marketplace?

- Is providing extra cash compensation consistent with the organization's culture?

- Can extra cash compensation help the organization manage compensation costs?

- Is the organization able to plan and set objectives effectively?

- Is the board willing to commit the time and effort needed to set objectives and to rate the chief executive annually in terms of those objectives?

- Will the board be able to act fairly, critically, and impartially in rating the chief executive?

SIGN-ON AND RETENTION BONUSES

Sign-on and retention bonuses are still relatively rare in nonprofit compensation, although not completely unknown. One recent survey found, for example, that 7.5 percent of the organizations in their survey provided some form of retention bonus.[36]

Each type of bonus can be a useful part of a compensation package: A sign-on bonus can provide an immediate inducement for changing jobs, while a retention bonus can encourage a long-term commitment to the organization. If a sign-on or retention bonus is part of the initial chief executive contract, it is protected from the intermediate sanctions regulations by the initial contract exception so long as the amount is fixed. However, no bonus is protected from the scrutiny of press, public, or staff. Since both types of bonus can represent a substantial expense to the organization, both must be fully justified in terms of the organization's needs.

---

36. Buck Consultants. *2002 Not-For-Profit Compensation and Benefits Survey.* p. 13.

SETTING UP A BONUS OR INCENTIVE PROGRAM

1. Engage all stakeholders in the program.

   • For many nonprofit organizations, bonus programs are controversial. The compensation committee should engage stakeholders when considering a bonus plan because their buy-in to both the existence and the design of the plan is essential.

2. Determine what purpose the bonus or incentive program will serve.

   • To improve organizational and chief executive performance?

   • To provide a more market-competitive salary?

   • To serve as a retention or deferred compensation vehicle for the executive?

3. Determine how the bonus program will fit into the compensation and benefits plan and market competitiveness.

4. Determine the level of the bonus relative to base salary and benefits.

   • The combination of base salary, bonus, and benefits needs to be consistent with the desired market position of the organization, and it cannot exceed comparable compensation practices in order to avoid intermediate sanctions issues.

   • A bonus cannot easily be added to base salary if base salary is already relatively high in comparison to the marketplace.

   • Bonus frequency and levels should be weighed against those of comparable organizations in the marketplace.

5. Determine the performance metrics appropriate for the bonus award.

   - How quantitative should the metrics be?

   - How can mission success be measured?

   - What metrics might raise questions relative to the organization's mission or with stakeholders or the public? For instance, commissions tied to fundraising are not acceptable in many sectors.

6. Determine the process for setting performance goals and reviewing results.

   - What role will the board play?

   - What role will the chief executive play?

   - How will the board assess performance and assign a bonus amount?

7. Determine the plan design.

   - Level of bonus as a percentage of salary or a fixed dollar amount.

   - Bonus range based on performance or a fixed dollar amount.

   - How the bonus is paid relative to the number of performance goals.

8. Identify the source of funding for the bonus plan.

Deferred Compensation

The term *deferred compensation*[37] is used to cover two overlapping categories of future compensation. In the broadest sense, deferred compensation refers to a portion of an executive's salary that is deferred for payment at some time in the future. This type of deferred compensation is simple ordinary income; the chief executive's contract should spell out the amount promised and the conditions, such as tenure and goal achievement, attached to its payment. In addition, the term deferred compensation is also used to refer to certain compensation arrangements that defer pay, tax free, until retirement or some other vesting time.

A nonprofit might have one or more reasons for including deferred compensation, broadly defined, in its chief executive compensation package:

- Deferred compensation can be an important part of an organization's compensation strategy. The vesting period linked to a deferred compensation plan can provide an incentive for the chief executive to stay in service to the organization; for example, a chief executive's contract might specify a cash payment if the chief executive stays with the organization for three years. The cash payment is often calculated as a percentage of annual base salary multiplied by the number of years in the deferral period. Future payments can also take the form of long-term incentives that are contingent on the achievement of certain goals.

- Deferred compensation can also help meet the chief executive's need for future income, especially in retirement. The special tax provisions described below are used principally, although not exclusively, for retirement-oriented deferred compensation. Retirement-oriented deferred compensation plans can be structured so they also support organizational goals, such as retention or the achievement of key performance objectives.

Deferred compensation arrangements are often complex and can have major tax and liability implications for both the organization and the chief executive. The chief executive and the board should both retain legal counsel when negotiating an agreement on deferred compensation. The brief description provided here of tax provisions and their possible advantages is no substitute for detailed advice from an experienced professional. For those organizations that may compete for talent with the for-profit sector, deferred compensation, even at the more modest and constrained level available for nonprofits, may help in partially leveling the playing field.

Tax-Deferred Compensation

Tax-deferred compensation is most frequently used as a way of preparing for retirement. Before considering special plans for the chief executive, the compensation committee should ensure that it provides salary deferral opportunities to its entire staff through a 403(b) or a 401(k) plan. These plans allow both salary deferral and additional employer contributions for retirement. 501(c)(3) organizations and public education employers are allowed to establish 403(b) plans; all employers other than state or local governments may establish 401(k) plans. Contribution limits under

---

37. Gregory L. Needles, Esq. and Boyd J. Brown, II, Esq. "Retirement Plans and Deferred Compensation for Tax Exempt Employees." Paper presented at Georgetown University Law Center Continuing Legal Education: Representing and Managing Tax-Exempt Organizations, April 25-26, 2002.

both types of plan are the same: elective deferrals of up to $14,000 in 2005, $15,000 in 2006; a combined limit of $41,000 on employee and employer contributions; or 100 percent of compensation. Under recently passed laws, organizations eligible to establish a 403(b) may also establish 401(k) plans. Organizations with both types of plan allow contributions to both.

Even when an organization has in place a savings plan for the organization as a whole, the chief executive may want additional opportunities for retirement savings because of the limits on the amounts that can be saved under a 403(b), 401(k), or 401(a) defined benefit plan. In addition to the absolute limits on the amount that can be contributed, the amount of salary that can be considered in calculating allowable contributions under qualified plans is capped at $205,000. 401(k) and 403(b) plans are also subject to nondiscrimination rules that can limit the amount that employers can contribute on behalf of legally defined highly compensated employees such as the chief executive. The nondiscrimination tests for 403(b) plans are somewhat simpler than those for 401(k) plans, and churches and government entities are exempt from the nondiscrimination test requirement.

Special deferred compensation plans for retirement are common among larger and more complex nonprofits, although they remain a minority practice among nonprofits in general. In one 2003 national nonprofit survey, 19 percent of chief executives surveyed had a deferred compensation or retirement plan in addition to standard defined benefit or defined contribution plans.[38] Since this survey includes only national organizations, the percentage of all U.S. nonprofits with such arrangements is probably somewhat lower.

The two principal nonqualified vehicles for tax-deferred compensation are designated by their Internal Revenue Code sections: 457(b) and 457(f). They are called "non-qualified" because they are not officially recognized as retirement plans by the IRS.

457(b) Plans

Under recent changes in the tax law, nonprofit employees may now defer income tax-free by participating in a 457(b) plan as well as a 401(k) or 403(b). 457(b) plans are limited to senior staff members (as a rule of thumb, no more than 10 percent of total staff) and hence are a variety of "top hat" plan. The contribution limit for 457(b) plans is the same as that for 401(k) and 403(b) plans: $13,000 for 2004, rising in $1,000 increments to $15,000 in 2006. Therefore, by creating a 457(b) plan, a nonprofit organization with an existing 401(k) or 403(b) plan can double the amount of compensation its senior employees can defer free of taxes.

Unlike 401(k) and 403(b) plans, which are the property of participating employees, a 457(b) plan is legally the property of the employer and is subject to creditors' claims until such time as it actually becomes available to the participant or beneficiary. Funds from a 457(b) plan cannot be distributed until separation from employment, or in the event of serious unforeseeable emergency.

A 457(b) plan can either allow the organization to increase compensation to senior executives in a way that defers taxes, or allow senior executives to defer more of their current salaries. In order to provide this latter option, therefore, organizations may wish to establish 457(b) plans even when they do not intend to use them to

---

38. PRM Consulting. *2003 Management Compensation Report: Not-for-Profit Organizations.* See page 133 for data on the number of chief executives with SERP or other plans.

provide additional compensation to senior staff. Alternatively, payments to a 457(b) can be tied to the achievement of annual or long-term goals, and thus serve as a retention and/or incentive vehicle as well as means of saving for retirement.

457(f) Plans

Nonprofits may also establish 457(f) plans. These plans have no limit on contributions, and taxes are deferred as long as the employee faces a legally defined substantial risk of forfeiture. The substantial risk of forfeiture generally takes the form of a vesting schedule, such as a promise to continue employment for a certain number of years. Such a schedule can, and often does, serve as the vehicle for a retention incentive or reward for performance; receipt of the 457(f) funds is contingent on fulfilling the requirement. The IRS takes the substantial risk of forfeiture requirement very seriously — a chief executive who leaves early does in fact forfeit the 457(f).

Once the substantial risk of forfeiture ends — for example, when the employee has completed the contract term — the full amount of the amount deferred is taxable. This can create substantial tax liabilities for a chief executive in the year of vesting. To mitigate this, organizations have taken several more or less creative approaches to delaying vesting, such as creating a rolling vesting period. The more creative the approach, however, the more likely the plan will face IRS scrutiny.

Some organizations explicitly fund their 457(f) plans, while others simply promise to pay at some point in the future. Like 457(b) plans, 457(f) plans legally belong to the organization and are subject to the claims of creditors.

457(f) plans are much more complicated than 457(b) or other saving and retirement vehicles. Both the organization's board and the chief executive should understand the conditions of the 457(f) plan, the risk of forfeiture, and the tax consequences of vesting. Drafting and review of the plan by an experienced lawyer and accountant is essential.

SPLIT DOLLAR LIFE INSURANCE PLANS

Some nonprofits have used the so-called split dollar life insurance plan as a nonqualified deferred compensation vehicle. Under a split dollar plan, the nonprofit pays either all or the majority of the chief executive's personal life insurance policy premiums. Ownership of the life insurance policy is split between the chief executive and the organization. The organization pays the premiums and is entitled to receive the value of the premiums upon the death of the employee. The employee or the beneficiaries receive the earnings on the premiums advanced.

The IRS has been skeptical about split dollar life insurance plans. Under regulations issued on September 17, 2003, split dollar life insurance plans are no longer a suitable instrument for deferring taxes. While in some cases an organization might still be interested in a split dollar plan as a life insurance vehicle, it should seek experienced legal advice before adopting such a plan.

Deferred compensation can be an attractive part of a compensation package, both for an organization and for its chief executive. It can support retention and encourage achievement of performance goals while helping a chief executive save for retirement. Providing further opportunities for tax-deferred compensation through increased funding of a 457(b) or through a 457(f) can make sense in some circumstances, especially for chief executives at the higher end of the market. Sophisticated and experienced legal and accounting advice is essential in considering such options.

As noted previously, all deferred compensation must be taken into account in determining total compensation for purposes of the intermediate sanctions regulations. Deferred compensation will also be reported twice on the organization's IRS Form 990: once in the year earned, and then again when it vests. For some organizations, this may generate undesirable impressions in the public eye.

OTHER BENEFITS AND PERQUISITES

Nonprofit organizations offer a range of benefits and perquisites to their chief executives. The value of the benefits packages generally range from about 10 percent to 25 percent of base pay, depending on the size and type of the nonprofit organization. Benefits values reported in IRS Form 990 filings tend to vary by organization type. Among larger nonprofits, benefits for chief executives can range from 15 percent to 25 percent, including deferred compensation.[39] Each organization's compensation committee must make its own decision as to what mix of benefits and perquisites makes sense by looking at market practice, the organization's culture and history, and the types of activities in which the chief executive is expected to engage.

Nearly all organizations provide the standard health insurance benefits, and many also provide disability and a modest amount of life insurance. Smaller organizations can often find cost-effective approaches to providing insurance through local nonprofit associations that have group plans.

A number of other benefit and perquisite possibilities also exist (please see the following page for a list of options). The authors recommend that compensation committees avoid including those that are less common in their chief executive compensation packages unless the inclusion of one or more will result in a demonstrable benefit to the organization.

Benefits, including the market value of such things as housing and transportation, must generally be included in the intermediate sanctions calculation. Perquisites can be a lightning rod for public scrutiny, and compensation committees should be very careful before approving anything that may seem out of the ordinary, excessive, or inappropriate to the culture and history of the organization.

---

39. Quatt Associates. *2004 Not-for-Profit Compensation Survey*. p. 9.

LIST OF BENEFITS OPTIONS FOR CHIEF EXECUTIVES

Relatively common benefits:

- Retirement benefits, either in the form of defined contribution plans, such as a 401(k) or 403(b) plan, or (now less common) a defined benefit pension plan

- Supplemental life, health, and disability insurance

- Memberships in professional organizations and subscriptions to professional journals

- Annual physical exams

- Car or transportation allowance

- Parking privileges

Specialized situation benefits:

- Housing allowance (including low-interest or no-interest mortgage loans), maintenance, and utilities: Most common among nonprofits such as colleges and universities whose chief executives are expected to entertain donors frequently, and organizations in areas with high costs of living

- Sabbaticals: Most common in educational and religious organizations

- Entertainment budget: Most common among larger nonprofits whose chief executives are expected to do extensive networking and entertaining on the organization's behalf

- Tuition assistance: Most common in the college and university environment, but can be provided by other types of nonprofits

Less common or emerging benefits:

- Social club or country club memberships (common among trade associations but not among charities)

- Financial counseling

- First class air travel

- Spouse travel

- Excess liability insurance

- Higher (or no) cap on long-term disability (this is very rare)

- Long-term care insurance

THE FINAL COMPENSATION PACKAGE

The compensation committee puts together the initial version of the organization's chief executive compensation package, but the final package will be based on negotiations between the full board and the candidate for the position. A wise board will enter those negotiations armed not only with knowledge of what the market allows, but also with a sense of the compensation elements it will be comfortable with in negotiation and the limits on negotiation of those elements.

- Beyond base salary, is the board open in principle to incentive compensation, and does it feel capable of administering an incentive system?

- Does the organization need a more sophisticated deferred compensation arrangement, and does the board want to bear the legal and accounting costs of establishing such a system, not to mention the possible costs in terms of public scrutiny?

- What benefits and perquisites has the organization traditionally provided, and how far beyond tradition might it be willing to go?

Asking and answering these questions beforehand will make for a clearer and more open negotiating process with the new chief executive and a higher level of comfort with the final package.

9.
Term Negotiations and Final Contracts

The final step in the chief executive compensation process is to establish the terms of the chief executive's employment, including the final form of the compensation package, and then formalize the relationship in writing. A formal and detailed written contract is desirable, but smaller nonprofits not wanting to go to the legal expense of drafting a detailed agreement should still put together a written memorandum of agreement that lays out salary, benefits, and date of employment.

NEGOTIATING EMPLOYMENT TERMS

The terms of employment are based on the job description and compensation package developed by the compensation committee, with adjustments negotiated by the full board and the candidate for the position. Both the board and the candidate need to prepare for these negotiations in specific ways. The following lists will be helpful in preparation for making the necessary adjustments.

THE CANDIDATE

Find the right fit

- The candidate should understand the needs of the organization, including its mission, objectives, and culture, and determine his or her ability to meet those needs.

- The candidate should understand what is expected in terms of position responsibilities and performance objectives.

- The candidate should determine if the organization is the best fit with his or her interests, skills, and preferred career path.

THE BOARD

Find the right fit

- The board should identify the needs of the organization based on its review of organizational strategy and objectives, and its understanding of the organizational history and culture. It should recruit and prescreen candidates based on those needs.

- The board should explain its expectations for the chief executive in terms of position responsibilities and performance objectives.

THE CANDIDATE	THE BOARD
Understand the role of compensation in the organization	**Understand the role of compensation in the organization**

THE CANDIDATE

Understand the role of compensation in the organization

- The candidate should ask the board its view of compensation and the role compensation plays in the organization.

- The candidate should understand the constraints that the organization's financial status, history, and culture put on compensation level and structure.

- The candidate should understand, if possible, the organization's current compensation practices, including base salary levels, increase practice, and incentive practice (if any), and use 990 data to learn how the previous chief executive and other high-level employees were paid.

THE BOARD

Understand the role of compensation in the organization

- The board should define the role of compensation in the organization (its compensation philosophy) and understand what constraints the organization's financial status, history, and culture put on compensation level and structure.

- The board should consider public and stakeholder scrutiny of its chief executive pay practices.

THE CANDIDATE

Understand the marketplace

- The candidate needs to understand the marketplace — what organizations similar in size, location, and mission typically pay, and how the pay is structured in terms of base pay, bonuses and incentives, and typical benefits and perquisites.

THE BOARD

Understand the marketplace

- The board needs to understand the marketplace — what organizations similar in size, location, and mission typically pay, and how the pay is structured. Understanding the marketplace will also enable the board to determine how the intermediate sanctions regulations may limit compensation.

THE CANDIDATE

Understand options for compensation

- The candidate should ask the board for its initial concept of how the compensation plan will work, including base salary increase plan, incentive compensation, and benefits.

THE BOARD

Develop options for compensation

- Based on the organization's financial status, needs, and culture, and the marketplace, the board should make an initial determination of how compensation will be structured, how the chief executive's performance will be measured, and what linkage there will be between pay and performance.

- The board should prepare a draft compensation plan, including a base salary range and expected benefits. It may also include performance-based compensation and a plan for annual salary increases.

THE CANDIDATE

Understand compensation requirements

- The candidate should understand his or her compensation and benefits needs, ranking them in order of importance.

- The candidate needs to understand the long-term financial implications of the compensation options in relation to his or her financial needs. The candidate may wish to engage a financial planner.

THE BOARD

Understand compensation requirements

- The board should discuss the candidate's compensation requirements with the candidate.

THE CANDIDATE

Contract

- The candidate needs to determine whether a contract is desirable from his or her perspective. A formal contract can clarify the expectations of both parties. The protection of a contract can be especially useful for the chief executive, who will clearly understand how the salary and incentive (if any) will be managed, how performance will be assessed, and severance practice.

- If a contract is required by the organization, the candidate needs to understand the terms of the contract.

- Legal assistance for the candidate can be helpful in negotiating the contract.

THE BOARD

Contract

- The board needs to determine whether a contract is desirable. A formal contract can clarify the expectations of both parties, and is especially helpful in laying out the process for salary adjustments, performance measurement, bonus and incentive practices, and severance practice.

- Compensation structure and level should be reflected in the contract. The contract should include starting salary; process for adjusting salary, e.g., at board discretion or based on a preselected index; incentive or bonus levels and process; and severance provisions, including termination policy, required notice, severance payment, benefits continuance, and others.

- Drafting the contract requires the assistance of an attorney.

THE CANDIDATE

Good Will and Flexibility

- The candidate needs to determine how flexible to be in the salary negotiation. What is the minimum acceptable salary? What benefits are essential? How can salary and benefits or perquisites be traded off?

- Salary negotiations should be conducted in good faith, positively and professionally. This is the beginning of what is hoped to be a long and productive relationship. Too contentious or confrontational a contract negotiation can get the relationship off on the wrong footing.

THE BOARD

Good Will and Flexibility

- The board needs to determine how flexible it can be in the salary negotiation. What range of salary is it open to? Which options are acceptable, and which are unacceptable?

- Salary negotiations should be conducted in good faith, positively and professionally. This is the beginning of what is hoped to be a long and productive relationship. Too contentious or confrontational a contract negotiation can get the relationship off on the wrong footing.

WRITING THE EMPLOYMENT CONTRACT

Many nonprofit organizations never take the final step of formalizing the relationship with the chief executive in a written contract. As of 2002, only one-fifth of nonprofits had formal employment agreements with their chief executives,[40] and a 2003 survey of larger foundations found that only 34 percent of their chief executives had contracts.[41] However, the authors encourage organizations to draft a formal employment contract or memorandum of agreement, even in the simplest employment relationships. Having a formal written agreement is advantageous for a number of reasons:

1. It makes the details of the compensation arrangement clear; together with the compensation committee's documentation of its decision-making process, it thus provides support for the reasonableness of the chief executive's compensation.

2. It provides a job description that outlines what the chief executive is expected to do, how and how often performance will be evaluated, and how compensation is tied to job performance.

3. It provides insurance that the terms that were discussed in negotiations will be honored.

4. It demonstrates the organization's commitment to the chief executive.

In short, a formal contract provides security to both the chief executive and to the organization and its board. By laying out the job description and compensation terms in writing, it ensures that mutual expectations are clear from the outset of the relationship. Even in the absence of a formal and detailed contract, we urge, as noted above, that the organization create a written summary of the terms of employment.

The contract will typically be drafted by the organization's in-house attorneys, if it has them, or by outside counsel. The chief executive candidate may also be represented by counsel in the drafting of the contract, but this is not always the case.

A typical contract includes the essential terms of employment. The following box lists all of the elements that might be included; the contract for a specific nonprofit will include only those that form part of its particular chief executive compensation package.

See Appendix II on page 62 for a sample chief executive contract that includes most of the items listed in the box that follows.

---

40. Buck Consultants. *2002 Not-For-Profit Compensation and Benefits Survey*. p. 60.

41. Council on Foundations. *2003 Grantmakers Salary and Benefits Report*. p. 44.

ELEMENTS TO INCLUDE IN AN EMPLOYMENT CONTRACT FOR CHIEF EXECUTIVES

- **The term of the contract and provision for contract renewal:** A term of three to five years is most common, but longer or shorter terms are possible.

- **A job description:** This may be attached as an appendix.

- **The starting salary**

- **Salary adjustment terms:** A schedule for future salary levels over the life of the contract, or language explaining how the salary will be adjusted going forward, such as increased according to the market, increased by a certain percentage, or increased at the discretion of the board based on performance and the market.

- **Incentive plans and performance bonuses:** How the incentive or bonus will work and how the incentive or bonus amount will be determined.

- **Retention bonus:** The amount to be paid if the chief executive stays for a certain term, either as a single amount paid at the end of the contract or as a stepped retention bonus with an amount paid out at stages over the life of the contract.

- **Retirement benefits**

- **Evaluation:** How often, how, and by whom the chief executive's performance will be assessed.

- **Deferred compensation:** This may be covered in the retirement plan.

- **Benefits and perquisites:** Health and other insurance coverage, as well as other benefits provided as part of the overall employment agreement.

- **Reimbursement of expenses:** Types of expenses that will be reimbursed, and the terms of reimbursement.

- **Noncompetition agreement:** Such an agreement prohibits the executive from engaging in private consulting work that may compete with the work of the organization. Upon the executive's departure, this agreement may also set restrictions on future business dealings as well as restrictions on whom the executive may hire away from the organization.

- **Confidentiality clause:** Ensures that any nonpublic information that is confidential or privileged to the organization will not be made publicly available.

- **Conflict-of-interest provision:** Describes potential conflicts of interest and indicates ways of preventing such conflicts.

- **Termination clauses:** A provision stipulating *with cause termination* releases the chief executive without severance benefits. With cause termination is often a result of legal wrongdoing. Contracts that stipulate without cause termination allow organizations to release the executive for poor performance or other related reasons, but the organization is typically obligated to pay severance benefits with termination.

- **Severance provisions:** This may be part of the contract or may be a separate document. Often designed to reflect the number of years served, such as one month's salary for every year of service.

- **Arbitration:** How conflicts over the contract will be resolved.

- **Governing law:** Identifies the state or jurisdiction under whose law the contract will be interpreted.

SEVERANCE

Letting a chief executive go is one of the most difficult challenges for a nonprofit board. In the absence of a contractual provision or other stated policy, the board is under no obligation to provide severance benefits to the chief executive.

If there is a severance policy it is typically set out as part of the chief executive's contract. A severance policy has several purposes:

- It may be necessary, since many chief executive candidates want severance provisions spelled out before accepting a position.

- It can serve as a retention vehicle for the chief executive, since voluntary departure may not trigger severance.

- It is common market practice and therefore contributes to the competitiveness of the compensation package.

- It reduces risk for both the chief executive and the board.

- It assures the candidate that, if the needs of the board change, the candidate will have time to look for other work. This helps compensate candidates for the risk they take in leaving their current positions.

- It assures the board that if its needs change or the chief executive falls short of expectations it can look for a new chief executive without causing undue harm to the current incumbent.

- It can help minimize any bad feeling between the former chief executive and the organization, as well as protect the organization from unfavorable publicity or legal action over claims by either party. The severance agreement will typically include a legal waiver and a promise of confidentiality.

Severance pay is a fairly common benefit among nonprofit organizations; a recent survey of national nonprofits conducted by PRM Consulting found that 41 percent of them provided severance packages.[42] A typical severance package includes the following provisions:

- Notice provision: Allows the board to terminate the chief executive at its discretion so long as it gives appropriate notice (30 days notice is common).

- Termination for cause: Allows the board to terminate the chief executive for cause without any notice. For cause generally means in the event of fraud or dishonesty, conviction of a felony or other major criminal offense, or failure to perform the duties of the position.

- Severance payment: Typically either a flat amount (e.g., six months or a year's pay); an amount based on length of service (e.g., two weeks for every year served); or a combination of the two (e.g., six months plus one month for every year served). There is often a cap on total severance: one year or 18 months of pay are common.

---

42. PRM Consulting. *2003 Management Compensation Report: Not-for-Profit Organizations.*

- Outplacement services

- Continuation of benefits for a certain period of time

- House repurchase or relocation assistance

- Nondisclosure

- Legal waiver of any claims

- Nondisparagement of the organization

- Future cooperation

No board wants to contemplate the possibility of its chief executive failing to meet expectations, or of its relationship with the chief executive becoming negative or unproductive. However, such things do happen, and a written contract and severance policy can be immensely helpful if and when they do. By putting in writing all of the terms for the chief executive's employment and dismissal, the board ensures that it will be able to manage difficult situations if they do occur, and protects the investment of time and resources that it has made in the complex process of developing its chief executive compensation package.

Conclusion

The chief executive compensation package is an important component of a board's responsibility to the nonprofit it governs, and putting the package together is a complex activity. For this very reason, however, it provides the board with valuable opportunities.

Chief executive compensation is tied to who the chief executive is expected to be as a professional, as well as to what the chief executive is expected to do for the organization. Setting the chief executive's compensation thus gives the board an opportunity to review the organization's mission, priorities, and goals in order to define the attributes that it seeks in a chief executive and the objectives that it wants the chief executive to accomplish. It also gives the board an opportunity to review the marketplace in order to determine what chief executives at similar organizations do and how they are compensated. By taking advantage of these opportunities and documenting its work, the board ensures that its chief executive compensation decisions will be in compliance with the legal requirements related to private inurement and intermediate sanctions.

Chief executive compensation, along with other financial management practices at nonprofits, has become the subject of intense public scrutiny. The compensation package cannot be hidden; it is reported on the organization's tax returns, which are available in the public domain. Setting the chief executive's compensation thus gives the board an opportunity to think about the organization's public image and the ways in which the chief executive compensation package can affect it, either positively or negatively. It also gives the board an opportunity to review the compensation structure across the organization. By taking advantage of these opportunities and maintaining an appropriate degree of transparency, the board assures the organization's staff that the chief executive's compensation is part of a coherent compensation structure for all employees, and assures the organization's donors and volunteers that the organization's finances are being handled wisely and well.

In every nonprofit organization, whatever its mission, history, or size, chief executive compensation is an important oversight responsibility for the board. Small nonprofits are subject to the same legal standards as medium-sized and large ones, including intermediate sanctions. To ensure compliance while making the development of the chief executive compensation package as productive a process as possible, all boards need to remember the following basic guidelines:

1. Establish a clear process for setting chief executive compensation, defining the steps in the process and who will be responsible for each.

2. Review the organization's mission, priorities, and goals and align the chief executive's role and compensation with them.

3. Develop a job title and a clear job description, and profile the characteristics and skills that a candidate must have to be successful.

4. Develop a compensation philosophy that accords with the organization's overall philosophic orientation and mission.

5. Gather information about the marketplace of comparable organizations in order to know what levels and types of compensation are appropriate and what candidates are likely to expect. Regardless of the organization's size, the chief executive compensation plan should be consistent with — and not exceed — the market. The IRS intermediate sanctions regulations require organizations with $1 million or less in gross annual revenue to use compensation data from three comparable organizations in the same or similar communities for similar services; larger organizations must draw data from the larger marketplace. To reduce the burden of finding and using market information, look to local or regional associations for information that is available for free or at low cost, and use Guidestar for free information on compensation practices.

6. Obtain professional advice to ensure that the chief executive compensation package will meet the "front page test" as well as legal standards. Recruit a board member or other stakeholder who is familiar with compensation practices and can provide assistance. Pro bono or low cost assistance from attorneys and compensation consultants is often available through local nonprofit associations, as well as through professional organizations such as Lawyers for the Arts.

7. Keep the compensation plan as simple as possible, and the process of developing it as transparent as possible.

Following these guidelines will not guarantee that board members will never have to answer questions about chief executive compensation; the compensation package is part of the board's responsibility and one of the elements for which the board is accountable to the organization's stakeholders and the general public. However, a board that follows these guidelines and the process outlined in this book will have a far easier time responding to any questions that are raised, whether by the IRS, the press, or the organization's donors and other stakeholders. Additionally, and perhaps more significantly, the members of the board will know that they have done their best to fulfill their responsibility to the organization they serve.

Appendix I

Using Consultants

Compensation consultants can help boards understand the market and assist them in negotiating the complexities of executive compensation plans. A compensation consultant is a neutral advisor who can offer knowledge and experience gleaned from many different organizations. By using a consultant who is experienced in and knowledgeable about nonprofit compensation practices, the board can receive additional assurance that it properly understands the marketplace and its options for setting compensation. The prospective chief executive can also be assured that he or she is being paid at a level that is appropriate to the marketplace.

Some nonprofit organizations might, therefore, be well served by a compensation consultant. However, final responsibility for establishing, monitoring, and ensuring the appropriateness of executive compensation rests with the board.

If you decide to use a compensation consultant, the first step is to determine the expertise the organization needs. The consultant should have experience in designing chief executive compensation for the nonprofit sector and ideally for the organization's particular part of the nonprofit sector. The consultant should have a good understanding of base salary, incentive, and deferred compensation options. He or she should fully understand, and have experience with, the intermediate sanctions regulations.

One of the best ways of assessing these qualifications is through references and referrals from other similar organizations. The references should cover the following:

- Timeliness and good project management

- Ability to work with staff, senior management, and the board

- Integrity, commitment, and technical competence

Once a consultant is hired, the lines of reporting and responsibility should be made clear. While the consultant may work closely with the organization's staff, the consultant's client should be the board, and the board should designate a single contact or small working group to manage the relationship. The board should then give the consultant a clear and complete project plan and access to relevant documents and information.

It is the consultant's duty to present the board with a comprehensible and competent analysis and recommendation. The board member(s) working with the consultant must provide adequate instructions and feedback to ensure that the product delivered by the consultant meets this standard. The consultant should also be available to meet with the full board to explain all findings and recommendations once they are made.

Fundamentals of the Board-Consultant Relationship:

1. Prospective consultants may be identified by the compensation committee or another subcommittee, but the full board should be involved in making the final selection.

2. The compensation committee or other designated members of the board should give the consultant direct guidance on what is needed.

3. The board should use the consultant as a resource as fully as possible, asking what the consultant thinks, what the consultant would recommend, and what the consultant believes are the advantages and disadvantages of taking a particular action under consideration.

4. The board should use the consultant to probe and challenge members' assumptions, and should also probe and challenge the consultant's assumptions.

5. Designated members of the board should review drafts of the consultant's reports before they are presented to the full board for consideration.

Appendix II

SAMPLE CHIEF EXECUTIVE CONTRACT*

Readers are encouraged to use this contract as an example only, to gain insight and guidance. Individual boards and organizations should create a contract according to the specific circumstances they are facing, and in doing so, should seek legal advice and review for any written agreement.

This Agreement is made between the ABC NONPROFIT (ABC) and NONPROFIT EXECUTIVE (Executive), for mutual consideration, the receipt and adequacy of which is acknowledged by the parties, who agree:

1. **Term.** Executive is engaged by the ABC Board of Directors to serve as Executive Director of ABC for a three (3) year period from January 1, 200X to December 31, 200X (subject to the terms of paragraph 6 below). This contract, if mutually agreed by ABC and Executive in their sole discretion, may by December 31, 200X be extended for an additional one (1) year period following successful completion of and positive performance reviews during both of the first two years of the contract. Provided that positive performance reviews continue in subsequent years, the contract, if then mutually agreed by ABC and Executive in their sole discretion, may be extended for one additional year following each positive performance year and, if so agreed, a contract with a term of two (2) years would exist at the commencement of each calendar year (subject to the terms of paragraph 6 below).

2. **Duties.**

   a. Executive will exert his full time and energy to his duties as the Executive Director of ABC. His duties and responsibilities as Executive Director are as customarily performed by a person in such position and as specified in ABC's bylaws, any position description for Executive Director, ABC's rules, policies and other governing documents, by ABC's Board of Directors, and by this Agreement. Executive is the chief employed officer who shall act at all times with a fiduciary duty to ABC. Executive reports to the Board of Directors and on a day-to-day basis he reports to the President of ABC.

   b. Executive shall work in the (City X) area as designated by ABC.

   c. Executive shall be responsible for developing and recommending to ABC's Board of Directors the annual budget and staffing plans. Executive shall have the authority to hire, supervise, evaluate, and terminate all ABC employees based on the approved staffing plan.

3. **Performance Evaluation.** Evaluation and assessment of the performance of Executive shall be conducted on an ongoing basis by the ABC President and ABC's officers, resulting in a formal written evaluation at least annually, prior to the anniversary date of this Agreement. The evaluation shall be based on an annual performance plan to be mutually developed by Executive and ABC's President and officers. The annual performance plan shall provide for and

---

* Adapted and reprinted with permission from Pfau Englund Nonprofit Law, P.C. For more information, please visit www.nonprofitlaw.com, call 703-304-1204, or e-mail spfau@nonprofitlaw.com.

assess performance of the general management of ABC and measurable goals and objectives for ABC and the Executive Director, taking into account the financial and staff resources made available by ABC. The annual performance plan shall be completed no later than the third month following the anniversary date of this Agreement. In the event that Executive's performance is found to be unsatisfactory, the ABC President shall describe in writing, in reasonable detail, specific examples of unsatisfactory performance. Upon the conclusion of the annual evaluation, ABC's governing board, in its sole discretion, shall determine the amount or type of increase in the salary and/or benefits of Executive to be made for the upcoming contract year.

4. **Salary and Benefits.**

   a. The base salary of Executive is payable at the annual rate of One-hundred Thousand Dollars ($100,000). After the first year, Executive shall be entitled to an annual cost of living adjustment to base salary based on the COLA provided to federal workers which, in addition to any merit increases awarded in the sole discretion of ABC, create an annual base salary rate.

   b. Executive shall be entitled to the following paid benefits: (i) a contribution to a pension plan acceptable to ABC at a rate equivalent to the annual rate of 10% of salary; (ii) annual leave at the rate of 15 days the first year, and at the rate of 20 days for each of the next two (2) years (with no more than two (2) weeks eligible for roll-over and use in any year). A maximum of two (2) weeks annual leave will be compensated at the expiration or termination of this contract; (iii) paid holidays at the rate of eight (8) days per year (on days to be determined by Executive consistent with his duties and responsibilities to ABC); (iv) sick leave at the rate of one (1) day per month, with a maximum of 200 hours of accrued but unused sick leave during the full-term of this contract; (v) personal leave at the rate of three (3) days per year; (vi) bereavement leave at the rate of three (3) days in the event of a death in the immediate family of Executive or his spouse; (vii) health insurance under a preferred provider organization selected by ABC, for single, individual coverage; (viii) life insurance in the amount of two (2) times the salary of Executive; (ix) disability insurance selected by ABC in its sole discretion; provided, however, that no salary or benefits may be taken or accrued until they are earned. The salary and benefits identified in this paragraph 4 constitutes the entire payment and compensation by ABC for the services of Executive.

5. **Business Expenses.** ABC will pay or reimburse Executive for reasonable and necessary business expenses up to Ten Thousand Dollars ($10,000) incurred by Executive which are directly related to the performance of his duties of employment, including travel, professional memberships and professional development, subject to documentation by Executive and approval by ABC.

6. **Cancellation and Severance.**

   a. ABC may cancel this Agreement immediately in the event of the death of Executive or the dissolution of ABC.

   b. ABC may cancel this Agreement 12 work weeks plus one day after the onset of physical or mental disability that prevents the effective performance of his duties for 12 work weeks plus one day or more provided that after such cancellation ABC shall then continue to pay Executive's salary either (i) for one-hundred twenty (120) days or (ii) until the date when disability insurance coverage commences, whichever is sooner.

c. ABC may cancel this Agreement immediately if Executive engages in an act or omission of dishonesty, fraud, misrepresentation, conflict of interest, breach of fiduciary duty, or any act of misfeasance, malfeasance or moral turpitude. Upon cancellation, ABC must disclose to Executive the act or omission upon which the cancellation of this Agreement is based.

d. ABC may cancel this Agreement for other reasons, with or without cause, which need not be disclosed to Executive, by giving Executive thirty (30) days notice in writing, and then paying to Executive severance consisting of six (6) months salary plus one additional month salary for each year of completed service to ABC, a maximum of two weeks accrued but unused annual leave (but not accrued or other unused sick leave or any other leave), and the dollar value of six (6) months plus one additional month of all other benefits as described in paragraph 4. Payments shall be made on a regular twice-monthly basis during a period equal to six (6) months plus one additional month for each year of completed service to ABC.

e. Upon the expiration, cancellation or termination of this Agreement with or without cause, no accrued or other unused sick leave shall be compensated.

f. Executive may cancel this Agreement by giving ABC at least thirty (30) days advance notice in writing.

g. The content and procedures set forth in this Agreement (and not those set forth in any ABC handbook or manual relating to employees generally) govern this Agreement in general and its cancellation in particular.

7. **Successors.** This Agreement is binding upon ABC and Executive, their heirs, executors, administrators, successors, and assigns. Executive will not assign or delegate any part of his rights or responsibilities under this Agreement unless ABC agrees in writing to the assignment or delegation. In the event of any merger, consolidation or reorganization involving ABC, this Agreement becomes an obligation of any legal successor or successors to ABC.

8. **Indemnification.** ABC shall indemnify, hold harmless, and defend Executive against all claims arising against Executive, his heirs, administrators and/or executors in connection with his employment by ABC and as permitted by law. Executive shall immediately notify the President and legal counsel of ABC orally and in writing upon learning of any actual or threatened dispute or legal process and shall cooperate fully in any defense or action.

9. **Entire Agreement.** This Agreement contains the entire Agreement between ABC and Executive. It may not be changed or renewed orally but only by an Agreement in writing signed by the President upon prior Board of Directors resolution and by Executive. This Agreement supersedes and cancels all previous agreements between ABC and Executive.

10. **Headings not controlling.** The headings of sections of this Agreement are not controlling.

11. **Governing law.** This Agreement is governed by the laws of the [District of Columbia].

_____

Executive   Date

_____

President, ABC   Date

Appendix III

FAQs

GENERAL TOPICS

Q: What are the trends towards making nonprofit salaries competitive?

A: Nonprofit salaries have risen over the last decade, and at least among larger and more complex nonprofits, the gap in salary compensation between for-profits and nonprofits has certainly narrowed. Moreover, some pay practices, such as bonus and deferred compensation, formerly seen only in for-profit organizations, are now increasingly common in nonprofit organizations.

That said, nonprofit total compensation still lags behind for-profit pay, and probably always will. In part this is because nonprofits cannot offer equity or other lucrative forms of long-term compensation. The larger reason, however, is that external scrutiny, federal and state oversight, and the internal culture of nonprofits generally discourage the payment of very high levels of compensation. For many nonprofits, financial considerations are also significant limits on executive pay.

The bottom line: Many nonprofits are now *appropriately* competitive — paying enough to ensure they can hire the talent they need, but not so much that they risk violating the public trust that expects them to focus on their main responsibility, their mission.

Q: What issues that nonprofits face in compensation are the same as or different from those that for-profits face?

A: Both for-profits and nonprofits face the challenge of balancing the market for executive talent against their internal resources. Nonprofits increasingly are able to use many of the same tools as for-profits in paying their executives. They can use bonus and incentive pay if they wish, and are able to offer some forms of deferred compensation. As noted above, base salaries have risen in recent years.

Nevertheless, nonprofits continue to operate under stricter constraints than for-profit organizations. As a result, total compensation at nonprofits remains generally below for-profit levels. Nonprofits face stronger public scrutiny and special legal oversight, through the IRS intermediate sanctions rules and other legal limits on compensation. Nonprofits cannot offer some of the most lucrative features of for-profit compensation, such as equity. Deferred compensation is subject to different, and stricter, rules for nonprofits. Bonus plans are less common, and when they exist, generally not as rich. Many nonprofits are also restrained in their pay practices by their mission, their culture, and donor and community expectations.

Q: How do nonprofits determine salaries for chief executives?

A: This book lays out a step-by-step process for determining chief executive pay. Those steps include

- Reviewing, and if necessary revising, the chief executive title and job description

- Reviewing organizational strategy and objectives and understanding how they connect with chief executive objectives and compensation

- Developing a compensation philosophy to guide decision making

- Understanding and researching the appropriate marketplace

- Understanding and complying with legal requirements

- Understanding and meeting the test of public scrutiny

- Choosing the appropriate level and mix of compensation, including base pay, extra cash compensation (such as bonuses and incentives), deferred compensation, and benefits and perquisites

- Documenting the compensation process and decision

Q: How does budget size relate to the chief executive's salary?

A: Budget size and chief executive pay correlate to some degree, and budget size is one of the factors that should be looked at as part of any market analysis. Budget size is also a factor that should be reviewed as part of any intermediate sanctions analysis.

That said, budget size by no means perfectly correlates with chief executive pay. Staff size, location, mission, the needs of the organization, its history and culture, and the qualifications and record of chief executive candidates can all affect chief executive pay in ways that swamp the budget size connection.

BOARD RESPONSIBILITY

Q: Should the entire board be aware of and/or approve the chief executive's salary and benefits each year?

A: The entire board should be aware of the chief executive's salary and benefits. A board may choose to seek advice from an outside expert when considering in detail and approving the chief executive salary and benefits. Only independent board members, however, should be involved in the final approval process.

Q: Our board has not historically approved the chief executive's salary and benefit package. We currently do not know specifics, so we need to get that information. Is it acceptable to ask the director to give us his salary, cost of health insurance, pension, and other information?

A: Generally there is a formal board process for receiving information about executive compensation. This information is typically provided either to the board chair, the executive committee chair, the compensation committee chair, or to the entire executive committee or compensation committee. The board, either in its entirety or through a delegated committee, is responsible for setting chief executive pay. It cannot do its job without knowing the full details of chief executive compensation. Staff must provide this information on request — usually through the already established board governance process.

Q: Can the board limit what it is willing to pay for a chief executive position and indicate that certain benefits are not negotiable?

A: Yes. The board is responsible for setting chief executive compensation, and for setting limits on what it will pay, or what benefits it will or will not consider. Of course, the board must also accept that its position may mean it cannot hire certain candidates.

LEGAL ISSUES

Q: Which laws should the board be familiar with when setting the chief executive's salary?

A: Board members need to be familiar with the IRS intermediate sanctions rules and related legal doctrines, such as the private inurement doctrine. They also need to understand the state law applying to their nonprofit. If the board considers deferred compensation arrangements, it needs to understand the federal tax law governing such arrangements. See our discussion of legal issues in Chapters 6 and 8.

Q: What is the IRS text on intermediate sanctions?

A: The intermediate sanctions rules are included in Internal Revenue Code Section 4958. The Internal Revenue Service *Instructions for Form 990* includes an informative discussion of the intermediate sanctions regulations. (See www.irs.gov/instructions/ for more information.)

Q: Are 501(c)(6) organizations included in intermediate sanctions?

A: Intermediate sanctions apply only to 501(c)(3) and 501(c)(4) organizations. Internal Revenue Code Section 4958 details the application of the intermediate sanctions rules. Other types of tax-exempt organizations, including 501(c)(6) organizations, are covered by the closely related private inurement doctrine, which also prohibits excessive compensation. See Chapter 6 for a further discussion of intermediate sanctions and related doctrine.

Q: Are chief executive pay records public information? What about the pay of other employees?

A: Chief executive pay, including cash pay and benefits, must be reported on the annual IRS Form 990 that almost all tax-exempt organizations must file. Pay for officers and the top five paid nonofficers must also be reported. IRS Form 990s must be made available to the public upon request.

OVERALL COMPENSATION

Q: How much money should a chief executive make? Should it exceed the combined salaries of the rest of the employees?

A: There is no single answer to how much money a chief executive should make. Chief executive pay should be consistent with that of the appropriate marketplace (as the IRS guidelines implementing the intermediate sanctions rules put it, the pay should be set at the "value that would ordinarily be paid for like services by like enterprises under like circumstances"). This book explains in detail how to determine an appropriate market salary for a chief executive. Boards also, of course, need to review the financial circumstances of the organization; it is impossible to pay at the market if the organization cannot afford it.

As for the chief executive's pay relative to that of other employees, as a general rule chief executive pay is 60 to 70 percent above that of the next highest paid employee. It would therefore be unusual to see chief executive pay higher than the combined salaries of other employees, and so large a differential might have an impact on employee morale. But without knowing the market for the chief executive and the duties of the other employees, a definitive answer to this question cannot be given.

Q: *Can you give me a list of the common compensation surveys?*

A: A list of representative national surveys, as well as some regional and specialized surveys, is included in the Suggested Resources at the end of this book. Each organization should also look carefully for local and regional survey data, and for survey information for organizations of its type. Such information may be available from an association representing similar nonprofits.

PERFORMANCE EVALUATION AND INCENTIVE-BASED COMPENSATION

Q: *We are in the process of evaluating our chief executive. How do we link this to compensation?*

A: The best way to link compensation to performance is to decide *before* the evaluation the rewards associated with achieving your organization's objectives. Thus, you could agree with the chief executive that achieving stated objectives would mean (finances allowing) a certain percentage increase in salary, or the award of an incentive amount. Going beyond the objectives would be worth more.

In the absence of an existing link between pay and performance, the next best thing is to decide on an appropriate reward (a salary increase, an ad hoc bonus, or some combination of the two) and carefully explain to the chief executive the particular achievements that justify the boost in pay. That explanation could then serve as the basis for the following year's performance plan.

Remember that any bonus or salary increase must not increase compensation by so much that it creates intermediate sanctions concerns.

Q: *Is incentive-based compensation for the chief executive of a nonprofit legal?*

A: Yes, incentive-based compensation for the chief executive of a nonprofit is legal, and it is an increasingly common practice among nonprofits. Many nonprofits find incentives an effective way to link chief executive pay to organizational performance and objectives. The total amount of compensation, including the incentive, must be consistent with market practice, however, to meet the intermediate sanctions and related legal standards.

Q: *My board chair and I would like to know what is common practice, or what options exist, for building in merit raises/bonuses for chief executive contracts. How do other nonprofits handle this? Is it put in the contract? Is it tied to performance?*

A: It is not uncommon for chief executive contracts to include guidelines for merit raises and/or bonuses. The contracts will generally either provide a mechanism for adjusting pay or provide for regular increases or bonuses at board discretion. Pay might, for example, increase annually by the salary movement in your area as reported by an authoritative survey source. Incentives could be linked to the achievement of certain objectives, or to the chief executive's remaining on the job for a certain number of years.

Even when the mechanism for adjusting salaries and providing bonuses is included in a contract, the board usually retains some discretion in adjusting the amount awarded on the basis of performance and/or the organization's financial status. Contracts with incentives will often specify the incentive amount but leave it to the board to establish organizational goals and assess the chief executive on the attainment of those goals.

Q: Is it common, or ethical, for the chief executive to receive incentive compensation based on the amount of money brought in?

A: Revenue-based incentives are not common and are considered unethical by many nonprofits. Organizations should be very cautious in linking fundraising to compensation because some donors may feel such arrangements are unethical. One way to avoid any possible appearance of unethical behavior is by having an organizational size objective rather than an explicit fundraising objective. It is also good practice to make revenue only one of several objectives; see the discussion in Chapter 2 on the balanced scorecard approach to objective setting.

From a legal standpoint, compensation arrangements that are at least in part based on the revenues of the organization are permissible under intermediate sanctions so long as their total amount is reasonable. Boards should consider the maximum amount that might be earned under such arrangements; the authors strongly recommend including a cap on compensation under such arrangements in order to ensure compliance with the law.

Q: Our chief executive is compensated by percentage of revenue; the salary is getting out of hand. What is a legal cap on executive compensation?

A: The legal cap, as laid out in the intermediate sanctions rules and related legal doctrines, is that "excess" compensation cannot be paid — i.e., more than is justified by the benefit the executive brings to the organization and by the compensation practices of "like organizations" in the marketplace. This text explains in detail how to determine excessive compensation under intermediate sanctions.

A percentage compensation arrangement is a red flag for intermediate sanctions purposes. Such arrangements are not barred by the regulations, but they may trigger special scrutiny for the reason alluded to above — total compensation may grow beyond market levels. The authors recommend including a cap on compensation based on reasonable total compensation in the related marketplace.

BENEFITS

Q: I think our chief executive receives too many benefits. How can I determine this?

A: From a legal perspective, the key issue is the amount of total compensation, which means base pay plus any incentives and benefits. That amount should be compared to the market, as explained in Chapter 5. Assuming the total amount of pay is reasonable when compared with the market, your next step would be to review standard survey data, which will typically include information on the prevalence of particular benefits. A review of such data can help you decide if your organization's practices are out of line with the market. Ultimately, however, the decision on what is appropriate will require weighing the cost of the benefits and other payments that your organization makes to the chief executive against the chief executive's value to the organization.

Q: Do nonprofits offer sabbaticals?

A: While sabbaticals are not a common benefit among nonprofits in general, some nonprofits, especially in the educational and religious sectors, do offer them.

Q: Our organization provides an automobile for the chief executive, which she is able to use for her private needs as well. Is this acceptable?

A: A nonprofit organization may provide an automobile for the chief executive, and the benefit is a reasonably common one, especially among larger nonprofits. Personal use of the vehicle is, however, taxable income to the chief executive.

Q: Should we provide a small mortgage to our chief executive?

A: Housing assistance is a relatively uncommon, although not unknown, benefit among nonprofits. A number of colleges and universities, for example, provide housing to their chief executives.

Some nonprofits also provide low-interest or no-interest loans to their chief executives. The interest subsidy must be taken into account in determining the reasonableness of compensation for legal purposes. The interest subsidy may also be a taxable benefit to the chief executive. Some states (for example the District of Columbia) prohibit loans to nonprofit officers and directors.

Q: Do you have any statistics on severance pay agreements?

A: Severance pay is a fairly common benefit among nonprofit organizations. About 41 percent of organizations in one recent survey of national nonprofits provided severance packages.[43]

Q: Are signing bonuses frowned upon by donors, the IRS, or others? Can we hire someone at $65,000 per year and give him or her half up front and the rest later as a regular pay?

A: Sign-on bonuses are quite rare in the nonprofit world, but they are not unknown. As long as the total amount of compensation is not excessive, there should be no IRS concerns; moreover, if this is genuinely an arm's-length initial contract, it should be subject to the initial contract exception to the intermediate sanctions regulations. The authors know of no ethical bar to the suggested arrangement.

CONTRACTING

Q: What are the advantages/disadvantages of chief executive employment contracts? How common is the practice? What should be included? What should be the duration?

A: Organizations should draft a formal employment contract in all but the simplest employment relationships. A formal contract provides security to both the executive and to the board, and makes absolutely clear the details of the compensation arrangement and the mutual expectations of the two parties. As of 2002, about one-fifth of nonprofits (19.5 percent) had formal employment agreements with their chief executives. The employment contract also offers some added security to both the

---

43. PRM Consulting. *2003 Management Compensation Report: Not-for-Profit Organizations.*

executive and the organization by demonstrating the organization's commitment to the executive.

The most important elements of a chief executive contract are listed in Chapter 8. A typical contract duration is three to five years.

Q: Do chief executives negotiate?

A: Of course they do. Boards need to negotiate, too. The authors hope that this book will help boards understand how to discover the appropriate pay and benefits for their organizations, and so give them the tools they need to negotiate effectively.

Appendix IV

GLOSSARY OF TERMS

Annual increase/raise — The yearly increase in base salary provided by most organizations, if allowed by their financial condition. Annual increases are generally a combination of a percentage increase reflecting inflation and an additional amount rewarding performance. Some chief executive contracts provide for annual base salary increases. This is done either at the discretion of the board or linked to market movement as reported in compensation surveys or government cost of living indices. Annual increases are also sometimes referred to as merit increases or cost of living increases.

Applicable tax-exempt organization — Intermediate sanctions regulations apply only to Internal Revenue Code 501(c)(3) public charities and 501(c)(4) social welfare organizations. These are called by the IRS applicable tax-exempt organizations. Other tax-exempt organizations are not formally subject to intermediate sanctions. They are, however, still subject to the private inurement doctrine, and a prudent board should act as if intermediate sanctions apply to its organization even if it is not a (c)(3) or (c)(4) by, for example, basing chief executive compensation on documented market practice.

Balanced scorecard approach — The balanced scorecard approach is based on the idea that financial performance measures alone do not necessarily ensure long-term organizational health. The balanced scorecard organizes objectives into four primary areas of performance: customer (or mission in the case of nonprofits), financial, internal, and innovation and learning. The balanced scorecard works especially well with nonprofit organizations as financial performance is not the primary criterion for organizational success.

Bonus — Compensation provided, often at the end of the year, in addition to regular base compensation. A bonus is generally provided as a reward for strong performance. A bonus can be part of a formal performance plan, or can be ad hoc. The terms *bonus* and *incentive* are sometimes used synonymously, but incentives are almost always linked to particular objectives, while bonuses may or may not be. Bonuses must be included as part of total compensation for intermediate sanctions purposes.

Conflict of interest — Individuals have a conflict of interest if they are on both sides of an actual or potential transaction.

Consideration — Consideration is a legal term meaning the bargained-for value exchanged between contracting parties. In the case of an employment contract, the consideration is typically service by the employee and compensation from the employer.

Correction period — The IRS provides for a correction period between the finding of an excess benefit under the intermediate sanctions regulations and the application of the second tier penalty (the first tier 25 percent penalty applies in any case). The correction period is, unless extended, 90 days after the date of mailing of a notice of deficiency (IRC § 6212). After the correction period, the second tier intermediate sanctions penalty applies — an excise tax set at 200 percent of the excess benefit.

Disqualified person — A disqualified person for intermediate sanctions purposes is someone who is in a position to exercise substantial influence with respect to the affairs of an organization subject to the intermediate sanctions regulations, i.e., an *applicable tax-exempt organization*. Disqualified persons include officers, key employees, board members, close relatives of officers and board members, and others in a position to influence the organization.

Excess benefit — An excess benefit is the economic value of any benefit received by a *disqualified person* that is in excess of the value he or she provides to the organization [see IRC § 4958(c)(1)(B)]. An example of an excess benefit is the amount of compensation provided to a nonprofit chief executive that is above reasonable market compensation for someone providing "like services by like enterprises under like circumstances."

Excess benefit transaction — For intermediate sanctions purposes, an excess benefit transaction is any transaction on the part of an *applicable tax-exempt organization* where the value of the benefit provided to a *disqualified person* is greater than any benefit the organization receives in turn [IRC § 4958(c)(1)(A)].

Fiduciary — A fiduciary is a person responsible for the administration, investment, and distribution of assets belonging to another person, or to an organization. The duties of the fiduciary are termed *fiduciary responsibility*.

Form 990 — IRS Form 990 is an IRS annual return that almost all tax-exempt organizations must file every year. The information on the form 990 must be made readily available to the public.

Incentive pay — Incentive pay is compensation paid in addition to base salary in response to the achievement of organizational or individual objectives. These objectives, and the amount to be paid upon the achievement of the objectives are generally specified in advance, often through a formal performance plan. Incentives may take the form of a percentage of a financial gain to the organization such revenue raised or cost savings achieved. Although the terms are sometimes used interchangeably, incentive pay differs from bonus compensation because it is linked to particular objectives, not to general performance. Incentive pay must be included as part of total compensation for intermediate sanctions purposes.

Independent board — An independent board is one that has no individuals who have a conflict of interest with regard to the person receiving or potentially receiving an economic benefit from the organization.

Initial contract exception — Under the intermediate sanctions regulations, the initial contract exception exempts transactions that are part of the initial relationship between an *applicable tax-exempt organization* and a *disqualified person*.

Insider — See *disqualified person*.

Intermediate sanctions — Intermediate sanctions has come to be used as a short-hand term for the federal regulations barring excess compensation and other excess benefits for officers, key management employees, board members, and other insiders at certain tax-exempt nonprofit organizations. Intermediate Sanctions apply only to Internal Revenue Code 501(c)(3) public charities and 501(c)(4) social welfare organizations. In form, Intermediate Sanctions are federal excise taxes (IRC § 4958), which are imposed on *disqualified persons* who engage in *excess benefit transactions with applicable tax-exempt organizations*, and on organization managers who knowingly approve of such transactions. The sanctions are termed "intermediate" because they are between IRS inaction and revocation of the organization's *tax-exempt* status. Other tax-exempt organizations are subject to the private inurement doctrine, which imposes similar restrictions, but without the detailed excise tax and regulatory regime of intermediate sanctions.

Merit increases — A term used to refer to annual salary increases for the employees of an organization. Although termed merit increases, most or all of the annual increase is often a cost of living increase. Organizations do, however, often increase or reduce the amount of the merit increase based on an individual's job performance.

Percentage-based compensation — Percentage-based compensation is compensation that provides for the recipient to get a percentage share of a financial gain, e.g., an amount of revenue raised. Gain-sharing or other percentage-based compensation arrangements, including arrangements based on the revenues of the organization, are permissible under intermediate sanctions so long as their total amount is reasonable. However, there should be proportionate benefit to the organization from such plans. The authors recommend that boards be especially careful in assessing such plans for their consistency with the market.

Perquisites — Benefits provided to a senior official at an organization — a chief executive or board member, for example. Perquisites differ from other benefits in being restricted to the most senior persons in an organization. Generally, they are not a direct financial benefit and many, but not all, are relatively modest in cost. They can include special parking arrangements, provision of housing, club memberships, spouse travel, sabbatical arrangements, and others.

Private benefit doctrine — The private benefit doctrine prevents organizations from qualifying for a tax exemption if the organization operates to benefit private interests to more than an insubstantial extent. Unlike the private inurement doctrine, the private benefit doctrine is not limited to situations where the benefits accrue to an organization's insiders.

Private foundation — A type of charitable organization, generally characterized as (a) being a charitable entity; (b) often funded from a limited number of sources, such as an individual, a family, or a corporation; (c) operating from investment income rather than contributions; and (d) making grants to other charitable organizations rather than funding and conducting its own program(s).

Private inurement doctrine — Private inurement is the diversion of an organization's assets or income to persons, generally insiders, who have not earned or merited it. Federal tax law differentiates nonprofit organizations from for-profit organizations by forbidding private inurement. Under the doctrine, *tax-exempt organizations* cannot provide income or assets to persons with a significant relationship with the organization (insiders), for their private purposes, through, for example, unreasonable compensation.

Public charity — A public charity is an IRC § 501(c)(3) organization that receives support from a wide range of sources or meets other specific requirements, such as a church, school, or hospital.

Publicly supported charity — Publicly supported charities are those that are supported through public donations. This distinguishes them from *private foundations.*

Rebuttable presumption of reasonableness — The rebuttable presumption of reasonableness is a partial safe harbor under the intermediate sanctions regulations that shifts the burden of proof to the IRS in showing that there has been an excess benefit transaction if certain conditions are met. Three conditions are required for the rebuttable presumption of reasonableness:

1. The compensation arrangement must be approved in advance by an authorized body of the applicable tax-exempt organization, composed entirely of individuals with no conflict of interest with respect to the compensation arrangement.

2. The authorized body obtained and relied on appropriate data as to comparability prior to making determination.

3. An authorized body must adequately document the basis for its determination.

Revenue-sharing arrangement — In a revenue-sharing arrangement a person receives a payment from a tax-exempt organization based on the organization's income, for example, a commission. Compensation arrangements that are at least in part based on the revenues of the organization are permissible under intermediate sanctions so long as their total amount is reasonable. However, the organization should receive proportionate benefit from such plans. The authors recommend that boards be especially careful in assessing such plans for their consistency with the market.

Salary cap — An upper limit on salaries within an organization. A salary cap may reflect financial constraints, the organization's culture and mission, the wishes of donors and supporters, or a combination of all three. Maintaining a salary cap over time can be difficult if it prevents the organization from recruiting and retaining desired staff. A salary cap can also lead to salary compression if lower level salaries increase with the market and senior salaries do not. This can lead to poor morale and higher turnover among senior staff.

Salary freeze — A salary freeze holds salaries in place throughout an organization. It is generally imposed in times of financial difficulty. Like a salary cap — but even more so — a salary freeze can prevent an organization from recruiting and retaining desired staff.

Self-dealing — Self-dealing refers to transactions where someone is in a *fiduciary* relationship with an organization and acquires or makes use of property for his or her own benefit that belongs to the organization.

Social welfare organization — A social welfare organization is a tax-exempt organization that engages in social welfare, such as civic, activities and is organized under IRC § 501(c)(4).

Tax-exempt organization — A tax-exempt organization is exempt from one or more federal, state, or local taxes, most commonly income tax. IRC § 501(a) and IRC § 501(c)(1)-(27) describe most of the organizations that are exempt from federal income tax.

Suggested Resources

Organizations

BoardSource: Formerly the National Center for Nonprofit Boards, BoardSource is the premier resource for practical information, tools and best practices, training, and leadership development for board members of nonprofit organizations worldwide. BoardSource,1828 L Street NW, Suite 900, Washington, DC 20036-5114. 202-452-6262 or 800-883-6262. Fax: 202-452-6299. www.boardsource.org

Chronicle of Higher Education (CHE): CHE regularly publishes articles on compensation trends and issues. It also puts out an annual issue with salary data taken from 990s. The Chronicle of Higher Education, 1255 23rd Street NW, Suite 700, Washington, DC 20037. 202-466-1000. www.chronicle.com

Chronicle of Philanthropy: The *Chronicle of Philanthropy* is a sister publication of the Chronicle of Higher Education. The *Chronicle of Philanthropy* is the newspaper of the nonprofit world. It is the news source, in print and online, for charity leaders, fundraisers, grantmakers, and other people involved in the philanthropic enterprise. Chronicle of Philanthropy, 1255 23rd Street NW, Suite 700, Washington, DC 20037. 202-466-1000. www.philanthropy.com

College and University Professional Association for Human Resources (CUPA-HR): A good source for information on university practices. Publishes an annual Administrative Compensation Survey. CUPA-HR, Tyson Place, 2607 Kingston Pike, Suite 250, Knoxville, TN 37919. 865-637-7673. Fax: 865-637-7674. www.cupahr.org/surveys/salarysurveysinfo.html

Council on Foundations: A first-rate source for information on foundation practices in general. Publishes an annual Grantmakers Salary Report. Council on Foundations, 1828 L Street NW, Washington, DC 20036. 202-466-6512. Fax: 202-785-3926. www.cof.org

WorldatWork: Formerly the American Compensation Association. WorldatWork is a nonprofit professional association for human resources. It provides information on compensation, benefits, and total rewards. Membership is required. WorldatWork, 14040 N. Northsight Blvd., Scottsdale, AZ 85260. 877-951-9191. Fax: 866-816-2962. www.worldatwork.org

General Survey Data

Abbott, Langer & Associates: Abbot Langer publishes an annual report on Compensation in Nonprofit Organizations. Abbott, Langer & Associates, Inc., Dept. NET, 548 First Street, Crete, IL 60417. 708-672-4200. Fax: 708-672-4674. www.abbott-langer.com

ERI: Economic Resource Institute provides salary survey analyses, geographic differentials, wage surveys, executive compensation information, cost of living comparisons, prevailing wage studies, employee benefit data, and compensation and benefits training. The database provides mostly corporate data but includes numerous positions in the nonprofit world. ERI Economic Research Institute, 8575

164th Avenue NE, Suite 100, Redmond, WA 98052. 800-627-3697. Fax: 800-753-4415. www.erieri.com

GuideStar: An extensive national online database of nonprofit organizations, which provides Form 990 data free of charge. For more detailed analysis a fee is required. GuideStar also publishes an annual Nonprofit Compensation Report. GuideStar, 4801 Courthouse Street, Suite 220, Williamsburg, VA 23188. 757-229-4631. www.guidestar.org

Mercer HR Consulting: Mercer HR provides an annual Benchmark Database Executive Survey Report. The survey is comprised of mostly for-profit data but includes a nonprofit cut. Mercer Human Resource Consulting Inc., 462 South Fourth Street, Suite 1100, Louisville, KY 40202-3415. www.mercerhr.com

PRM Consulting: PRM publishes an annual national Compensation Survey of Management Positions for Not-for-Profit Organizations. PRM Consulting, Inc., 1814 13th Street NW, Washington, DC 20009. 202-745-3700. Fax: 202-745-3701. www.prmconsulting.com

Quatt Associates, Inc./PBS: In conjunction with the Public Broadcasting Service, Quatt Associates, Inc. conducts an annual survey of salary and benefits for major national nonprofit organizations. The survey is available to participants only. Quatt Associates, Inc., 2233 Wisconsin Avenue NW, Suite 501, Washington, DC 20007. 202-342-1000. Fax: 202-338-1000. www.quatt.com

Society for Human Resource Management (SHRM): SHRM is an association devoted to human resource management. It publishes both a Benchmark Compensation Survey and a Benefits Survey annually. Society for Human Resource Management, 1800 Duke Street, Alexandria, VA 22314. 800-283-SHRM (7476). Fax: 703-535-6490. www.shrm.org

Watson Wyatt: Watson Wyatt publishes an annual Top Management Compensation report. This survey includes mostly for-profit data, but a nonprofit cut is provided as well. Watson Wyatt, 1717 H Street NW, Washington, DC 20006. 202-715-7000. Fax: 202-715-7700. www.watsonwyatt.com/research/

REGIONAL SURVEY DATA

A number of regional surveys are available. Examples include the Cordom Associates Nonprofit Organizations Salary Survey for the Washington, DC area; the Louisiana Nonprofit Salary and Benefit Survey put out by the Louisiana Association of Nonprofit Organizations; and the Colorado Nonprofit Salary & Benefits Survey put out by the Colorado Association of Nonprofits.

Visit www.fundsnetservices.com/grantman.htm for a more complete list and contact information.

Education

American Council on Education (ACE): ACE's Publication, *The American College President*, provides demographic and salary data from all sectors of American higher education. American Council on Education, One Dupont Circle NW, Washington, DC 20036. 202-939-9300. Fax: 202-833-4760. www.acenet.edu

Association of Governing Boards of Universities and Colleges (AGB): One Dupont Circle NW, Suite 400, Washington, DC 20036. 202-296-8400. Fax: 202-223-7053. http://data.agb.org/. Membership required.

CUPA-HR: College and University Professional Association for Human Resources. The Association publishes an annual Administrative Compensation Survey. CUPA-HR, Tyson Place, 2607 Kingston Pike, Suite 250, Knoxville, TN 37919. 865-637-7673. Fax: 865-637-7674. www.cupahr.org/surveys/salarysurveysinfo.html

Museums

American Association of Museums (AAM): AAM is the resource for compensation issues in the museum field. AAM produces the annual American Association of Museum Directors Salary Survey as well as other surveys on museum compensation and benefits. American Association of Museums, 1575 Eye Street NW, Suite 400, Washington, DC 20005. 202-289-1818. Fax: 202-289-6578. www.aam-us.org

Philanthropic Organizations

Council on Foundations: The Council publishes an annual Grantmakers Salary and Benefits Report. The Council on Foundations, 1828 L Street NW, Washington, DC 20036. 202-466-6512. Fax: 202-785-3926. www.cof.org

New York Regional Association of Grantmakers (NYRAG): NYRAG is a nonprofit membership organization for philanthropy in the NY metropolitan area. NYRAG publishes an annual Compensation Summary of its member organizations. New York Regional Association of Grantmakers, 505 Eighth Avenue, Suite 1805, New York, NY 10018. 212-714-0699. Fax: 212-239-2075. www.nyrag.org

Trade Associations

American Research Company (ARC): ARC publishes an annual National Compensation Study of Association Chief Executives. This is a highly detailed source that focuses exclusively on trade association chief executives. American Research Company, Inc., 10003 Robindale Court, Great Falls, VA 22066. 703-759-3188. Fax: 703-759-3127. www.AmericanReseachCo.com

American Society of Association Executives (ASAE): The Association publishes an annual Executive Compensation and Benefit Survey. American Society of Association Executives, The ASAE Building, 1575 I Street NW, Washington, DC 20005. 888-950-2723 or 202-371-0940. Fax: 202-371-8315. www.asaenet.org

Greater Washington Society for Association Executives (GWSAE): GWSAE publishes an annual Compensation Survey for trade associations, professional societies, and charitable nonprofits, including some that do not have members in the greater Washington area. GWSAE is now a part of ASAE. GWSAE, The Ronald Reagan

Building and International Trade Center, 1300 Pennsylvania Avenue NW, Washington, DC 20004. 202-326-9550. Fax: 202-326-0999. www.gwsae.org

National Journal: The National Journal publishes a biennial survey of association chief executive salaries. The data are taken from Forms 990 or comparable sources. National Journal Group Inc., The Watergate, 600 New Hampshire Avenue NW, Washington, DC 20037. 202-739-8400. Fax: 202-833-8069. www.nationaljournal.com

Quatt Associates, Inc./Associations Human Resources Group (AHRG): In conjunction with AHRG, Quatt Associates publishes an annual survey of salary and benefits of major national trade organizations. The survey is available to participants only. Quatt Associates, Inc., 2233 Wisconsin Avenue NW, Suite 501, Washington, DC 20007. 202-342-1000. Fax: 202-338-1000. www.quatt.com

PUBLICATIONS

Albert, Sheila. *Hiring the Chief Executive: A Practical Guide to the Search and Selection Process.* Washington, DC: BoardSource, 2000. Hiring a new chief executive is one of the most important tasks a board must undertake. This book presents a model for the process that can easily be adapted by almost any nonprofit organization. It stresses the importance of legal advice, identifies the most important characteristics of the next chief executive, and provides valuable questions for the candidate-interviewing process. This revised version comes with a CD-ROM with sample forms to help your board screen and interview candidates.

Axelrod, Nancy R. *Chief Executive Succession Planning: The Board's Role in Securing Your Organization's Future.* Washington, DC: BoardSource, 2002. Chief executive succession planning is not only about determining your organization's next leader. It is a continuous process that assesses your organization's needs and identifies leadership that supports those needs. A successful succession plan is linked to your organization's strategic plan, mission, and vision. Author Nancy Axelrod helps board members prepare for the future by examining the ongoing and intermittent steps of executive succession planning.

Barbeito, Carol and Jack P. Bowman. *Nonprofit Compensation and Benefits Practices.* New York: John Wiley & Sons, 1998. This book provides an overview of current workforce, employment, and compensation trends in the private, government, and nonprofit sectors. In addition, it offers a detailed examination of innovative compensation practices, important guidance on establishing and implementing a competitive compensation plan, and real-world case studies.

Berry, Brian. *Strategic Planning Workbook for Nonprofit Organizations.* St. Paul, MN: Amherst H. Wilder, 1997. Strategic planning is a tool for finding the best future for your organization and the best path to reach that destination. This classic workbook gives you practical guidance through five planning steps. Useful step-by-step worksheets help you develop the plan, involve others in the process, and measure results.

Chait, Richard P., William P. Ryan and Barbara E. Taylor. *Governance as Leadership: Reframing the Work of Nonprofit Boards.* New York: John Wiley & Sons and Washington, DC: BoardSource, 2005. *Governance as Leadership* introduces a fresh way to think about governance, with sensible guidance to turn these ideas into concrete actions. The book will be particularly valuable to staff of professionally managed nonprofit organizations, and to others, including foundation officers, donors, consultants, and students of nonprofit organizations, who are interested in improving nonprofit governance.

Hopkins, Bruce R. *The Law of Intermediate Sanctions: A Guide for Nonprofits.* New York: John Wiley & Sons, 2003. This comprehensive, easy-to-use guide provides necessary explanations of the constitution and application of intermediate sanctions — fines and legal actions intended to eliminate nonprofit abuse. The text summarizes, analyzes, and explains the federal tax law on intermediate sanctions, addressing such topics as the statute, legislative history, regulations, and court opinions of intermediate sanctions; the influence of law concerning private inurement, private benefit, and private foundation self-dealing; real-world examples of intermediate sanctions in practice; and how nonprofits may seek to avoid excess benefit transactions or adequately document that excess benefit does not occur.

Mintz, Joshua. *Assessment of the Chief Executive: A Tool for Nonprofit Boards.* Washington, DC: BoardSource, 2005. By failing to adequately evaluate the chief executive, many nonprofit boards miss an opportunity to express support for the executive and strengthen his or her performance. Neglect can be costly, resulting in high turnover, mistrust, and ongoing poor performance. This resource provides a comprehensive tool boards can use in the evaluation process. After discussing the benefits of assessment, the user's guide suggests a process and provides a questionnaire that addresses every major area of responsibility. This tool is also available in online format, which guarantees faster and easer compilation of results.

Ober|Kaler, attorneys at law. *The Nonprofit Legal Landscape.* Washington, DC: Board-Source, 2005. Designed for executives and board members, *The Nonprofit Legal Landscape* explains the laws and legal concepts that affect nonprofit organizations. It serves as a handy reference tool for laws specific to tax exemption and for those regulating general business practices. When confronted with legal questions, nonprofit leaders can use this easy-to-read resource to rise rapidly to the next level of understanding.

Samuels, David G. and Howard Pianko. *Nonprofit Compensation, Benefits, and Employment Law.* New York: John Wiley & Sons, 1998. This reference book covers a broad range of employee-related issues confronting officers, directors, managers, and attorneys of nonprofit organizations. It provides an overview of such topics as intermediate sanctions, IRS audits, nonqualified arrangements, and the Age Discrimination in Employment Act. Also included are a discussion of church plans, a look at employee benefit aspects of mergers and acquisitions, and case studies.

Self-Assessment for Nonprofit Governing Boards. Washington, DC: BoardSource, 1999. BoardSource's proven assessment book is designed to help nonprofit boards determine how well they're carrying out their responsibilities and identify areas that need improvement. This evaluation toolkit includes a user's guide and 15 board member questionnaires so that you can easily distribute them to your board. This resource is also available in a quick and easy-to-use online version. Contact BoardSource for more details.

About the Authors

Brian H. Vogel is a senior principal with Quatt Associates, Inc., a Washington, DC-based management consulting firm specializing in nonprofit compensation, performance management, organization development, and strategic planning. Mr. Vogel's practice includes the design of staff and executive compensation and performance systems, and their review under the Intermediate Sanctions regulations and other legal requirements. He also works extensively in strategic planning.

Mr. Vogel is a graduate of Harvard College and Harvard Law School. He can be reached at bvogel@quatt.com.

Charles W. Quatt, Ph.D., is president and founder of Quatt Associates, Inc. Mr. Quatt specializes in executive compensation and performance management systems. He is nationally recognized for his work in nonprofit executive compensation and has extensive experience developing compensation and retirement plans for nonprofit executives. Mr. Quatt lectures regularly on nonprofit executive compensation, deferred compensation, and performance planning.

Prior to his management consulting engagements, Mr. Quatt served as a faculty member at Harvard University and Princeton University. He earned his Ph.D. from Harvard University. He can be reached at cquatt@quatt.com.